Blood Brothers

TEXAS A&M UNIVERSITY

26

MILITARY HISTORY SERIES

Blood Brothers

A Short History of the Civil War

FRANK E. VANDIVER

Texas A&M University Press : College Station

The paper used in this book meets the minimum requirements of the American National Standard for Permanence of Paper for Printed Library Materials, Z39.48-1984. Binding materials have been chosen for durability. ♾

Illustration credits:

All photographs are from the ten-volume set *The Photographic History of the Civil War, in Ten Volumes,* ed. Francis Trevelyan Miller (New York: Review of Reviews, 1912).

Maps 1 and 2 are by Barbara Long, from Frank E. Vandiver, *Their Tattered Flags: The Epic of the Confederacy* (1970; College Station: Texas A&M University Press, 1987). Maps 3 and 4 are from *American Millitary History,* ed. Maurice Matloff (1969; Washington, D.C.: Center of Military History, United States Army, 1985).

Engravings are from Robert Underwood Johnson and Clarence Clough Buel, eds., *Battles and Leaders of the Civil War,* volume IV (New York: Century Company, 1884).

Library of Congress Cataloging-in-Publication Data
Vandiver, Frank Everson, 1925–
    Blood brothers : a short history of the Civil War / Frank E.
    Vandiver.
        p.   cm. – (Texas A&M University military history series ;
26)
    Includes bibliographical references and index.
    ISBN 0-89096-523-4. – ISBN 0-89096-524-2 (pbk.)
    1. United States–History–Civil War, 1861–1865. I. Title.
II. Series.
E468.V36 1992
973.7–dc20   92-10985
                                       CIP

In memory of
THOMAS LAWRENCE CONNELLY,
Gallant Rebel

Contents

Illustrations

ILLUSTRATIONS

Acknowledgments

This book is an outgrowth of an assignment from John E. Jessup, editor in chief of the *Encyclopedia of the American Military,* to do a military survey of the American Civil War for that publication, to be published by Charles Scribner's Sons in 1992. I am indebted to Dr. Jessup and to the executive editor, Louise B. Ketz, for permission to use portions of my essay in this book.

One of the joys of working in the Civil War field is contact with helpful people. Through the months of writing, a good many friends helped, and a good many libraries made everything easier.

My research assistant, Edith Anderson Wakefield, did her usual outstanding job in checking references and quotations, in preparing statistics and organizing library loans far and wide. My able administrative assistant, Debbie Riley, worked diligently in preparing computer copy. My good friend Dr. Arthur Blair, cohort of long standing, sometime English professor, helped with his practiced listening ear.

I am especially indebted to the Sterling C. Evans Library of Texas A&M University for splendid help and for unstinting Library Loan support. Dr. Donald Dyal of the library's Special Collections provided particular help with the illustrations, as did Guy Swanson of the Confederate Museum in Richmond.

My special gratitude goes to my colleague, good friend, and former student, Prof. Walter Buenger of the history department, Texas A&M University, who read the manuscript in an early form and offered sound and most constructive suggestions for improvement. Thanks also to Prof. James I. Robertson, Jr., for extremely helpful reading of the manuscript and suggested corrections.

I reserve for the Texas A&M University Press particular appreciation for daring and confidence over considerable time. My editor, Mary Lenn Dixon, combines artistry with style, and my debt to her is profound and acknowledged with the pleasurable sense of finding a dear friend.

My family, as usual, put up with more about the Civil War than normal duty demanded. My wife, Renee, listened, cajoled, and sustained willingly and with love throughout long weeks of composition. My daughters, Nita and Nancy, and my son, Frank, listened to long snatches of prose by telephone with their usual patience. My stepson, Joseph Carmody, endured many hours of enforced quiet for a writer without complaint. My love and special thanks to all of them.

Much inspiration for this book comes from my graduate students who have listened and argued over the years. I have respectfully dedicated this book to one of them, the late Thomas Lawrence Connelly, a scholar and man of courage.

Blood Brothers

One War, Two Revolutions

Karl von Clausewitz once observed that nations will fight wars in ways resembling their social systems, and history seems to bear him out. Close viewing of the Civil War suggests a corollary: nations will fight wars in ways reflecting their leaders' personalities.

To unusual degrees, Abraham Lincoln and Jefferson Davis embodied their causes. A tale of joint lineage persisted for years, born from the similar looks of the two presidents and spurred by a kind of bar sinister possibility coming from nearness of birthplaces. Untrue, the story nonetheless did anticipate some similarities in ways of warring. Lincoln's rough-hewn western pragmatism set a tone for Northern war management that enabled a great, inchoate country to throw off the shackles of agrarianism, once conservative Southern lawmakers departed congress, and ultimately to make a revolution. Free at last to enjoy laws favoring industry and manufacturing by liberalizing credit and the money supply, laws sharpening individual power and responsibility, the North surged with new energy and finally waged a war not only to save the Union but also to make the Union far different than before.

Lincoln did not plan all these results; in fact, he started with the limited war aim of an intact Union. But he did not shy from war; he expected it, wanted it to come when it did—witness his comment, in a speech urging rejection of the Crittenden Compromise, that "the tug has to come and better now than later" (quoted in Charles P. Roland's *An American Iliad*). He meant to wage it fully to a firm and certain end. He feared from the outset that war might work its own harshness, perhaps become an unstoppable engine of change. Whether the war could be controlled, could be "civilized," depended on length and on severity. Which meant that a lot depended on the South's way of war.

When large Rebel armies took the field and fought toe to toe with large Union armies, the war grew beyond American memory into one of the world's greatest conflicts. When that happened, old ideas and methods warped into different dimensions. Society changed in radical ways as the North saw freedom as America's promise and slavery as a blight on the goal. Abolitionists seized on their chance to make a cause different from Union and to reshape society while recasting America's labor force.

Northern farmers, too, found new ways of working; traditionally they had been staple people, spurning the big crops of the slave ilk. Now they were to see themselves the grainers of the war effort and indispensable. Workers in the industrial areas, too, were indispensable, and they found new strength in organization—organization not always welcome to management or to certain downtrodden American workers like the Irish. But honor came to the laborer and was cherished. This newfound status made many Northern workers skeptical of black competitors, made them dubious allies of abolition. They saw freedmen as rivals for jobs. War measures bent old rules as the government invaded private lives and businesses, public areas and lands. As all these things happened, Lincoln's America vastly changed into a different, revolutionary power.

Jefferson Davis had a different America in mind from the start, an America of two selves. In his vision, the North would go on with industrialization, with reckless gobbling of space and resources, with the unfettered zeal of consumption; the South, accustomed to agriculture, to a slower way of business and society, to honest graciousness, and to slavery, would work its way to a different world. Davis and his fellow Rebels are often accused of dooming the South by turning backwards, away from progress. Not so. Southern leaders did not reject the future; they sought ways to accommodate its coming.

Davis and other Confederate leaders knew in their hearts that the Old South could not linger, no matter how much they wished it might. Not fools, they knew the strength of changes sweeping the western world – Britain's sea patrols against the slave trade, South American crusades for nationalistic liberalism, Canada's push for a free country. Cotton still was king, but a monarch threatened by democracy. The Confederacy came, not as a bulwark for the past but as a way to a different destiny. So subtle a point is lost in war; most Confederates fought because the North refused to acknowledge Southern "rights" and Yankees became invaders.

Like Lincoln, Davis feared, too, the changing power of a long war. And he expected a long conflict, one that might erode values and slough virtues. Such a price might be worth paying if an independent Confederacy emerged, committed to a Southern modernity.

LINCOLN'S NORTHERN WAY OF WAR

Under Lincoln's careful eye the North organized a massive effort and wielded it with increasing force. Under his eye, too, a lot of old verities went to the cauldron of conflict. Critics, and there were many arising during the war, complained that the Union's president paid lip service to freedom while acting like a tyrant. True, to some extent. As the war went on and crises compounded, new ways of coping had to be found. And Lincoln showed unusual, even uncanny, skill at coping.

William Seward, who became Lincoln's secretary of state, had the cockiness of arrogance and, in the beginning of Lincoln's administration, cherished some contempt for the bumpkin president who whittled through cabinet meetings with crude humor and uncertainty. Superiority led Seward to some incautious doings during the early months of false peace. His "negotiations" with Davis's commissioners brought no complaint from Lincoln, and that may have induced daring beyond trust. On April 1, 1861, the secretary forwarded to Lincoln an unusual document (collected by Henry S. Commager in *Documents of American History*, I, 392) titled "Some Thoughts for the President's Consideration." Seward deplored a lack of foreign or domestic policies in the crisis and proposed to avert civil war by shifting the issue from a matter of slavery to one of union or disunion – from chattels to patriotism. He suggested drumming up a war with Spain and

Abraham Lincoln, April 9, 1865, the day of Lee's surrender

France as a way of diverting the South from its course to one of sup-porting national interests. He proposed abandoning Fort Sumter be-cause it, somehow, had become a slavery symbol; at the same time he would defend vigorously all other forts and recall the navy to en-force a blockade. "There must be an energetic prosecution" of these policies, Seward said, and it must be "somebody's business to pur-sue and direct it incessantly. Either the President must do it himself, and be all the while active in it, or Devolve it on some member of his Cabinet. Once adopted, debates on it must end, and all agree and abide." Unctuously he announced, "It is not my especial prov-ince; But I neither seek to evade nor assume responsibility."

Lincoln caught the challenge and assessed it in light of the man. Seward had value in the cabinet because of his power in the party; his diplomatic skills were questionable, especially in light of his pro-posed foreign war and his unbridled hatred of the British. But he had the virtues of his failures: determination, devotion to the Union, fearless candor, and energy. Gideon Welles (Commager, *Documents,* I, 392) had tagged him accurately as a man who "liked to be called premier," as his "Thoughts" clearly indicated.

In a masterly reply, Lincoln corralled his secretary and kept a friend. Writing shortly after Seward left his missive at the White House, Lin-coln addressed the issue of policy or no policy. Looking back a month, he reminded the secretary of state that in his inaugural he had an-nounced that "the power confided to me will be used to hold, oc-cupy, and possess the property and places belonging to the Govern-ment. . . ." At the same time orders had gone to Gen. Winfield Scott to do everything possible to hold the forts. So, said the president, a policy much like the one Seward outlined had already been an-nounced, with the exception of abandoning Fort Sumter. As for some-one being in charge, Lincoln said, "I must do it. When a general line of policy is adopted, I apprehend there is no danger of its being changed without good reason, or continuing to be a subject of unnecessary debate; still, upon points arising in its progress I wish, and suppose I am entitled to have, the advice of all the Cabinet."

Seward found no change in attitude toward him. Knowing that he had in the secretary a true "hard war" man, Lincoln trusted him with tasks arising from an increasingly strong national effort. The presi-dent passed on to Seward a good many extracurricular problems, some of them even extra-constitutional. Most onerous among these was the matter of arbitrary arrests for treason or threat of treason–usually of persons who spoke or wrote favorably of the Confederacy or in some way denigrated, or hampered, the Union cause. Again, Lincoln picked his man with unerring sense – probably no other high Federal officer would have attacked the problem of sedition so sedulously, so pointedly, and with such organization. Despite Lincoln's clear assertion of command, Seward continued to think like a grand vizier and hence surrounded himself with various totems of power – including a secret service organization willing to do his bidding all across the country. Arrests were widespread and brought bristling complaints, even from Att. Gen. Edward Bates, who resented having the court system embroiled in extralegal persecutions.

Lincoln, uncertain about the unity of the nation, gambled above the law while he worked to firm his cause. Instead of asking congress to suspend the right of habeas corpus in potentially disloyal areas, he simply suspended it by administrative fiat, which was most improper and most pragmatic. He avoided the court system by executive abrogation of civil liberties – by arresting many accused of aiding the enemy or of sedition, not charging them, and later simply letting them go.

What brought the matter to the glare of public view was the arrest of a civilian, John Merryman, by military authorities in Maryland. Caught recruiting for the Rebels and burning railroad bridges, he was cast into Fort McHenry dungeons, where he rested a thorn in the American judicial side. Championed by Justice Roger Taney, chief justice of the United States and also presiding judge of Maryland's federal circuit court, Merryman became a cause célèbre in the history of Anglo-Saxon civil liberties. Taney held his arrest illegal, since civil courts were functioning and had been bypassed. Nothing went more directly to the heart of American conscience than a case that smacked of military dictatorship. Deeply concerned, the president defended his actions at some length in his message to congress on July 4, 1861, and in several careful letters to concerned citizens.

For a lawyer-president, one steeped in the civil-libertarian tradition and its fervent western practice, the Merryman case hung heavy in the mind. Lincoln put the best face he could on presidential suspension of habeas corpus – the burgeoning emergency confronting the government. True as that argument was, a large outcry greeted it. Some prominent constitutional lawyers took the president's side; many, the other side, and an argument raged throughout most of the war. Lincoln continued to suspend the civil courts where he thought necessary and congress wisely avoided the issue as long as possible. In March, 1863, congress finally passed a law that approved what he had done.

Freedom of speech lingered a hard problem for a warring democracy. Unfortunately the matter invariably tangled with partisan politics. Republican local politicians, editors, and spokesmen regarded most Democratic comments, written or spoken, as treasonous ipso facto. Activities of several fairly disorganized groups such as the Sons of Liberty, Knights of the Golden Circle, and Order of American Knights became large and haunting conspiracies in Republican fancies. Typically, "secret" rites played against fears and magnified political agitation into "plots" against the Union. Although the "Copperhead" movement—a term usually applied to Democrats to symbolize seditious intent—did have some strength in Indiana, Ohio, and even Illinois, it represented more Democratic party shenanigans than intrigue for treason. Threats of a "Northwest Confederacy" were far more wishful than real.

Doubtless the most embarrassing, surely the most blatant, case of infringed freedom of expression involved an Ohio Democrat of some prominence, Clement L. Vallandigham. On May 1, 1863, he made a speech at Mount Vernon, Ohio, accusing Lincoln's government of frivolously prolonging the war, a war not for the Union but for the liberation of blacks and enslavement of whites. Under orders of Gen. Ambrose E. Burnside, commanding the Department of the Ohio, military authorities arrested Vallandigham and tried him by military commission—all this while civil courts were doing business. Pleased at sudden martyrdom, Vallandigham issued a ringing jail appeal to fellow Democrats: "I am a Democrat—for the Constitution, for law, for the Union, for liberty—this is my only 'crime.'"

Although probably approving Burnside's order, Lincoln saw the power of Vallandigham's protest; cabinet members advised a discreet retreat. Agreeing, Lincoln took the occasion to denounce halfway Democrats who, like Vallandigham, talked for their country with "'buts' and 'ifs' and 'ands.'" Extraordinary times required like measures, Lincoln argued publicly. The Constitution, he said, allowed actions in war not allowed in peace; the war transcended party in a "battle for the country we all love." Besides, said Lincoln in a deft aside, Burnside was a Democrat! He changed Vallandigham's sentence to banishment to the Confederacy—across which Vallandigham traveled swiftly, decamped by blockade runner, and went to Canada where he continued agitation against "tyranny."

Lincoln tried various ways to slip the snare of impaired free speech. But arrests of newspaper and magazine editors whose writings appeared to some officer somewhere as aiding the rebellion tarnished the administration's image. In February, 1862, Lincoln sponsored an order setting political prisoners free and transferred administration of arrests from Seward's zealotry to the war department, where a commission examined special cases. A presidential proclamation on September 24, 1862, sought to regularize military arrests by declaring that anyone discouraging enlistments, resisting conscription, or guilty of disloyal practices was subject to military trials. Far from controlling arrests, this proclamation encouraged them. How many were arrested? Estimates range from 40,000 down to 4,440, with a number somewhere around 10,000 seeming a likely best choice. What is important is the fact that relatively few people lost liberty because of opinions—many of the jailed were guilty of partisan politics, and that seems a less defensible reason. Yet politics continued, elections were held, opposition continued, even consolidated, and the Democrats emerged from travail a stronger, tighter party. So did the Republicans.

President Lincoln met overt obstructionism with force. Labor strikes in key industries were quickly repressed by troops. Draft riots posed difficult problems, because filling the ranks might well depend on how rioters were treated in various parts of the country. Riots erupted after the passage on March 3, 1863, of the Enrollment Act, consigning all fit male citizens between twenty and forty-five to the ranks—with exemptions, of course, and with the proviso that a substitute might be hired for three hundred dollars. On July 13 a smattering of orderly protesters appeared in New York City and quickly gave way to crowds of largely Irish unskilled workers—men, women, children (child labor was on the rise). The rioters raged the streets, burning draft offices and attacking draft officials and soldiers who tried to stop them. They sacked abolitionist homes and at last turned their fury on the city's blacks. Anarchy almost ruled. For the administration, New York's troubles had special portents. The mayor of the city, Fernando Wood, had secessionist leanings and talked of free city status for the largest city in the country. That kind of break would probably seal the Union's fate and could not be allowed.

After two steamy days the riots subsided, leaving a shocking toll of some 120 dead (many of them blacks) and 300 injured. A smoky pall over the city told a tale of wanton destruction. The rioters were not really against the war or for the Rebels—they were frustrated and fearful of a coming industrial giant that would freeze them firmly on the bottom of society.

Once the riots stopped—they were the worst in American history—Lincoln advised charity toward the rioters. Most grand juries refused indictments, and money was raised to provide substitutes for the army for poor workers who could prove hardship. Although the administration maintained its authority firmly, it showed mercy. Mercy followed necessity in this case—workers were too vital for general alienation.

Practicality governed presidential polices in most areas of civil conflict. Lincoln's pragmatic, some would suggest cavalier, attitude toward dissent provoked but did not stifle democracy. In fact, it has been argued that the hot discussions of civil liberties enriched appreciation of the Constitution as a document strong enough to sustain war in its own defense. Underlying this point are the plaints increasingly heard during the 1850s that the supreme law of the land lacked resilience, that the country and the times had passed it by. Lincoln's pragmatic warring above the document merely confirmed its utility.

Further evidence could be noticed in Lincoln's constant expansion of presidential war powers. He learned to use executive clemency politically—doling out pardons to suit the mood of the war—and kept a close eye on military justice. Although he finally had a highly competent war secretary in Edwin M. Stanton, Lincoln—like his Rebel counterpart—served mainly as his own minister of war. He struggled to find generals who could marshal the growing resources of the Union, organize them effectively, and hurl them at the enemy. In this search he encountered surprises, lethargy, varying war philosophies, and frustrations beyond belief.

Changes are always slow in war—daily emergencies dull the sharpest wits—but firepower did force changes in tactics. Combined with new transportation methods, both tactics and strategy would evolve to different dimensions. Lincoln had some knowledge of these technical changes, but turned to wise army heads for instruction. His relations with venerable Winfield Scott, the senior soldier of the Union, were cordial but tinged with realization that this veteran of the War of 1812 could hardly stand the stress of a wildly expanding modern war. Lincoln searched for another general in chief and settled on the dapper George Brinton McClellan, whose mein and measure seemed to suit him perfectly to the role of national savior. Time would show, though, that behind the spiffy tunic, the warrior's stern visage, beyond the image on the charger, McClellan lacked battle fire; he could organize brilliantly, parade with zest, but could not fight the army he burnished to such style.

So Lincoln kept strategy and "grand" tactics under his own untutored gaze—which bothered him because he knew his own martial inexperience. He had, he lamented, only slight exposure to fighting in the Black Hawk War, and that as a back country militia officer. After John Pope's failure in mid-1862, McClellan was restored to command because he could, at least, reorganize defeated men into an army. Barebones victory at Antietam and an escaped Robert E. Lee convinced the president that the Army of the Potomac must have another leader. Ambrose Burnside failed, as did Joseph Hooker, against Lee and the amazing Stonewall Jackson. George G. Meade at least won at Gettysburg, but, like his predecessors, seemed glad to let Lee go back to Virginia. Where was the man who knew the North had more of everything and knew how to use mass and materiel?

Out in the west an unheralded general named Ulysses S. Grant began to string victories together, to keep Rebel armies occupied and divided, and, at last, to rupture the Confederacy by capturing Vicksburg. Here might be the man. And he was—Lincoln made Grant commander of the armies of the United States early in 1864 and turned strategy and tactics over to an expert hammerer, who hung on to Lee's army while he urged Sherman to stick with Joseph Johnston's army and pushed other Union forces to menace all points so that Southern troops could not be shifted from one front to another. Lincoln caught the tactics in a good Illinois metaphor: those not skinning can hold a leg.

But until he found Grant, Lincoln tinkered with command structure and commanders, with plans and with recruiting to the point of irritating some of the good generals he had. What choice did he have? As Seward had said, "There must be an energetic prosecution" of the war, and Lincoln had said he, himself, would do it. So he did, in sound western style.

After McClellan's thin victory at Antietam, Lincoln seized the moment to change the nature of the war. On September 22, 1862, the president read to the cabinet the second draft of a document he had read them first in July: a proclamation of emancipation. When they had heard the contents earlier – although the cabinet knew his concerns about flagging patriotism, falling enlistments, and growing war weariness, his hope of shifting victory from more than saving the Union to freeing the bondsman – members had hesitated. Nothing touched more tender nerves than the whole issue of slavery and emancipation. Freeing the slaves by waving a presidential paper smacked of a dictator's direst deed.

Personally favoring emancipation, Lincoln did feel official obligation to go slowly. Democrats would object, but so would many Republicans and independents. More importantly, so would some border states, especially Kentucky, which Lincoln worked hard to keep loyal. The hard summer of 1862, with its list of Union military setbacks, plus a forced solution to the Kentucky problem, opened the situation. In Lincoln's mind slavery was the heart of the rebellion, and emancipation would suitably punish the slavocrats who had started the war. True, agreed the cabinet, but Seward had a good question about timing: would it not be better to wait for a sound Union victory before issuing the proclamation? Resting it on defeats would reduce its impact, make it sound like a wail for help from a dying cause.

That made sense. Lincoln would wait, but he knew he had to offer the Union, and the world, more of a cause than a vision of the United States before the war – that was gone up in carnage. Northern people recognized that and felt a floundering of purpose. Why were so many dying for a lost war aim? Freedom, though, remained the strongest of American urges, and freeing the slaves at least had the blessing of long struggle. Strictly as a war measure designed to catch the coattails of patriotism, the proclamation made sense.

But Lincoln had his own qualms. He did not forget his pledge in the first inaugural not "to interfere with the institution of slavery. . . . I believe I have no lawful right to do so, and I have no inclination to do so." He meant it then, but the war changed things. A conservative by nature, Lincoln felt the states had control of their social order; he wanted them to emancipate the slaves and even offered a congressional plan for compensated manumission in the border and loyal slave states that offered good monetary and time considerations. Meeting scant enthusiasm for the idea, a disappointed president came slowly to the realization that freeing the slaves might be the most important action he could take to aid the war. But he worried that decreed freedom for blacks would solidify Southern opinion; he clung to the thin hope of avoiding "a violent and remorseless revolutionary struggle" and tried to keep preservation of the nation as the main objective.

Cabinet fears were well founded. When he issued what he called the Preliminary Emancipation Proclamation on September 22, a storm of outrage burst over the White House. Numbers of Democrats were naturally appalled; many generals found themselves leading in a war whose purpose had changed to one they could not support. On January 1, 1863, Lincoln issued a formal proclamation and suffered louder denunciations. Whole legislatures screamed at Lincoln's incredible action. "Unwarrantable," said the Illinois House and Senate (with Democratic majorities), "a gigantic usurpation" that suddenly transformed the war into a

> crusade for the sudden, unconditional and violent liberation of 3,000,000 negro slaves; a result which would not only be a total subversion of the Federal Union but a revolution in the social organization of the Southern States, the immediate and remote, the present and far-reaching consequences of which to both races cannot be contemplated without the most dismal foreboding of horror and dismay. The proclamation invites servile insurrection as an element in this emancipation crusade – a means of warfare, the inhumanity and diabolism of which are without example in civilized warfare, and which we denounce, and which the civilized world will denounce, as an uneffaceable disgrace to the American people. (Commager, *Documents*, I, 422)

Content posed part of the problem. To almost everyone the documents rang hollow, full of changes for expediency. The Preliminary Proclamation gave the Rebel states until January 1, 1863, to get back in the Union without loss of slaves; after that, slaves would be freed wherever the Union held sway, save in loyal slave states. When the final Proclamation was issued in January, the glaring lapse of freedom could be seen by every reader. Slaves were declared free in rebellious areas, with the following exceptions: Tennessee, all the loyal slave states, and those portions of Virginia and Louisiana under Union control. In effect, no slaves were freed where Lincoln could have ordered them so. Earl Russell of England observed to the British ambassador in Washington that the document appeared strange, indeed, since it "professes to emancipate all slaves in places where the United States authorities cannot exercise any jurisdiction . . . but it does not decree emancipation . . . in any States, or parts of States, occupied by federal troops . . . and where, therefore, emancipation . . . might have been carried into effect. . . . There seems to be no declaration of a principle adverse to slavery in this proclamation" (quoted in J. G. Randall and David Herbert Donald, *The Civil War and Reconstruction,* p. 381).

Cynics might have observed that Lincoln's decree did, in effect, protect slavery from certain recent congressional attacks upon it made by confiscation acts in August, 1861, and July, 1862. Radical Republicans, an increasingly difficult wing of the party for Lincoln, pushed hard the idea that the war made no sense unless slaves were freed and argued, besides, that the Rebels made good use of them for military labor. That persuasive argument induced Congress to legislate the loss of Rebel property in land and slaves, simply for being Rebels – and Lincoln disliked the attainder features that carried punishment on beyond the doers. He wanted to veto the second bill, the toughest, but Radicals persuaded him to accept a limp compromise. In the end he had his way by not pushing the attorney general to enforce the law. And the Emancipation Proclamation, by putting the freeing of slaves under executive stamp, effectively took control from congressional vengeance.

Emancipation bothered Lincoln throughout the war; he wrestled with conscience, war necessity, and simple justice – and he supported it as "a fit and necessary war measure," he said, one that "otherwise unconstitutional, might become lawful, by becoming indispensable to the preservation of the constitution, through the preservation of the nation" (Randall and Donald, *Civil War and Reconstruction,* pp. 382–83). Lincoln never wavered; freedom for blacks became a nonnegotiable condition. He firmly supported passage of the Thirteenth Amendment to the Constitution, which would abolish slavery.

What of all these things done in the name of war? Were they necessities, or were they simply the deeds of an unconstitutional monarch?

Considered strictly in their own contexts, these actions do have imperial overtones. Seen, though, in the full sweep of Lincoln's view of the country, they seem far less threatening to American ideals. Freeing the slaves became an important war aim, but Lincoln's personal objective remained holding the nation together at virtually any cost. He explained that devotion clearly in a public statement replying to the "Prayer of Twenty Millions," an editorial urging a bold strike at slavery which Horace Greeley published in his New York *Tribune* on August 20, 1862. "My paramount object in this struggle," Lincoln's statement said, "is to save the Union, and is not either to save or to destroy slavery. If I could save the Union without freeing any slave I would do it, and if I could save it by freeing all the slaves I would do it; and if I could save it by freeing some and leaving others alone, I would also do that." This, the president said, reflected official policy, not his "*personal* wish that all men every where could be free."

Consider some of the legislation the president either advised or supported. Taxation remained a thorny problem during the war; in the beginning, as costs skyrocketed, some doubted the North could raise enough money to sustain the effort. But Salmon P. Chase, secretary of the treasury, tried methods beyond taxation. Borrowing had always been a main prop of the fiscal system; now it had to be expanded beyond old boundaries. Bonds were sold, not only to banks and the wealthy, but also to small investors. Chase turned to the private sector for help. He persuaded Philadelphian Jay Cooke to aid the national government.

Cooke, a wealthy banker who had sold bonds covering Pennsylvania's three-million-dollar 1861 loan, began an almost superhuman personal effort as bond salesman. Advertisements, prepared editorials, careful suasion of editors, published lists of "patriots" who contributed, night sales offices for worker convenience, even sermons from eager clergymen—all these avenues were used. As a modern student, Phillip Paludan, observes: "Such publicity helped to build the image of a united people rising in support of the cause" ("*A People's Contest,*" p. 117). Cooke's skills were measured in success. Right after the Battle of Bull Run he raised $2 million in Philadelphia alone; by August, New York financial houses had bought $35 million worth, and Boston bankers $10 million. Cooke employed agents who took a commission, but brought in so much revenue that few complaints of profit were heard.

Congress responded to a hard money secretary's plaints for revenue with a Legal Tender Bill on February 25, 1862. This authorized $150 million in non-interest bearing notes, which would be legal tender for taxes, internal duties, personal debts, and excises—everything but import duties, still payable in specie. That exception, plus the added promise of the government to pay interest on bonds and notes in specie, devalued the new money. Still, the bill made important changes by ending a government policy of using only gold or silver. The law would never have cleared a congress heavily loaded with laissez-fairist Southern Democrats. The "greenbacks," as these new notes were called, vied with a dizzying mass of paper issued by the government and by state and local banks in a kind of monetary chaos.

While many in congress still feared that greenbacks would ruin the country, the fact is that only $450 million worth were issued, and they did cause part of the inflation that doubled the cost of Northern living by January, 1865.

Costs of war continued unbelievably upward. A national debt of only $65 million in 1860 escalated to $90.5 million in 1861. By 1866 the debt reached the astronomical amount of $2,755,764,000, a fraction of the war's $13 billion cost.

Taxes brought in increasing amounts of cash, though the burden became heavy for many. On August 5, 1861, congress asked the states for $20 million through a direct land property tax. Tucked away in that bill lurked a bold and different path to fund raising: an income tax, the first in United States experience. All incomes over $800 per year were taxed at 3 percent. Congress lagged in enforcing the income proviso; no provision for tax collectors was made until mid-1862.

War, though, finally worked a fundamental revenue change in the North. An excise tax, enacted July 1, 1862, became the largest source of war funding; it raised ten times more money than the income levy. The excise tax hit small consumers hardest. They could not pass the cost along to customers, as did businesses, and they were hurt, too, by paying for items protected under tariffs. As Paludan says: "Greenbacks, taxation, and borrowing were all part of an integrated vision of the type of economy that the war made indispensable. All pointed to a more centralized and centralizing system. . . . Linked with these other measures was a proposal . . . for a national banking system to provide a uniform currency throughout the nation and hence reinforce public confidence in the economy" (p. 122). A complete revolution in financing happened because Lincoln allowed it – saw it as vital to victory and a legitimate use of war expediency.

War opened the way for all kinds of changes needed if the United States were to grow into a power for the twentieth century. Lincoln pushed not only the changes that fostered hard war, but also those which built a better country. Not really touted by historians as a social reformer, he nonetheless deserves high rank in that category. While war most occupied his mind and tongue, he did keep watch on such things as education, the lives of the poor, and the growth of business and industry into important pillars of economic power.

Federal support for education lagged before the war, despite the precedent of the Northwest Ordinance, which gave one section of land to every township in the Territory for common schools. But sentiment grew for increased agricultural training and increased education for the "industrial classes." Congress had passed a land grant bill in 1857 that would have created universities for practical education. Southern concerns about dangerous growth of governmental power, plus western desires to keep all profits from the public lands, all added to President Buchanan's constitutional scruples, and he vetoed the bill. With opponents gone for the nonce, with the need for greater public education clearly revealed by war's evidence, congress passed the Morrill Act in June, 1862. Surely the most important piece of legislation concerning education since the Northwest Ordinance, the Morrill Act gave thirty thousand acres of public land to every state for every senator and representative in congress. States poor in public lands were compensated by land they could sell. Proceeds from the sale of these tracts would support colleges "to teach such branches of learning as are related to agriculture and the mechanical arts," as well as military tactics. The act included future states and covered those temporarily out of the Union. Enthusiastic patriotism on Northern campuses, where a rush to enlist shrank student ranks heavily, helped the Morrill Act's passage. Lincoln had no constitutional qualms about aiding education and gladly signed the bill.

Gladly, too, he signed the Homestead Act passed in May, 1862, to go into effect on January 1, 1863 – an act that allowed any twenty-one-year-old loyal citizen or head of a family with little money to claim up to 160 acres of land. Now "little people" could buy cheap land. With expanding transportation, a flood of legitimate settlers might push speculators out of the western land business. Railroads were the key.

Precedent helped the president support grants to railroads for heavy construction projects. In 1850 the Illinois Central had benefited from the first land grant law – a law that had given big tracts of land which the railroad could sell to help build more miles of track. The State of Illinois had grown prosperous, and Lincoln remembered. Happily he signed the Union Pacific Railroad Bill in June, 1862, which provided huge land grants to two railroad construction companies to build a line between Omaha, Nebraska, and Sacramento, California –and so tie the Union together with a belt of iron. Some congressional grumbling greeted the 400-foot right of way and ten sections of land per mile (five on each side of the track)—altogether amounting to 15.5 million acres. Grumbling or not, congress doubled the grant in 1864 and offered loans in addition. In future years there would be much conflict because of these grants, but war required expansion of economic and political bases and congress acted quickly, without conscience for the future.

Lincoln himself never stopped looking toward the future. He supported funding new banks so that a national currency could flourish and felt that federal encouragement of commerce not only aided the war but strengthened the nation. And he thought of the nation after the war, of life in a reunited country, and so he worked for a peace of charity and welcome. "Reconstruction" occupied his mind from the beginning of conflict; his "ten percent plan," under which he hoped to win Louisiana and other states back swiftly, showed his cast of thinking. He did resent Rebels, even castigated "Bobby" Lee, lamented the waste rebellion levied, but saw forgiveness as the way to reconciliation.

Three things he did near the end of the war, and the end of his life, reveal his personal feelings. First, when he gave his second inaugural address in March, 1865, he spoke of the future, not the past, avoided vengeance or rebuke, and urged Northerners to "judge not that we be not judged." And he set the noblest goals for the victors. "With malice toward none; with charity for all . . . let us strive on to finish the work we are in; to bind up the nation's wounds . . . to do all which may achieve and cherish a just and lasting peace. . . ." Second, he visited Richmond on April 5, 1865, wandered the streets of the enemy capital without concern for safety, and visited the home of Gen. George Pickett. When informed that Pickett was with Lee, the president said to tell him his old friend Lincoln had stopped by. Third, a few nights later, when a Union army band came to serenade him at the White House and asked what he would like to hear, he answered "Dixie." It had been fairly won, he thought, and was a fine tune.

Just as an epic needs a hero, a great cause needs a vision, and Lincoln provided the vision that first justified all the war measures, then legitimized them, finally made them noble. He had glimpses of the vision before the war, before he stood higher than an Illinois office-seeker. It was slow in coming and blurred, but he tried to articulate some of what he felt as he debated the nature of the Union with Stephen A. Douglas in 1858. He kept at it until the red light of combat etched the vision clearly on a full and open heart. One part of what he saw concerned emancipation. When he tried to persuade congress to offer compensated freeing of slaves, he caught a fleeting view of what was coming. "*We* can not escape history," he told both houses on December 1, 1862. "The fiery trial through which we pass will light us down in honor or dishonor to the latest generation. . . . In *giving* freedom to the *slave* we *assure* freedom to the *free*. . . ." That same certainty led him to the Emancipation Proclamation, and when he changed the nature of the war, he changed himself.

From uncertain leader of an uncertain nation, he now grew to be the Great Emancipator. No matter the gaps in the call for freedom, the breaking of the chains rang round the globe. When he seized on circumstance to make slaves free, he freed himself from the past. On a new road to freedom a new war could run. As it did, he came more clearly to the vision of America. His own long struggle to find words to tell the beauty of the vision aching in his heart ended at Gettysburg, Pennsylvania, slightly more than four months after battle there. He saw it clearly now, "a new nation, conceived in Liberty, and dedicated to the proposition that all men are created equal." As he looked out on the crowd come to commemorate a great Union victory, he saw beyond the people, beyond the harrowed fields to the purpose of the war, a war to test "whether . . . any nation so conceived and so dedicated can long endure." The survivors must keep faith, must "resolve . . . that this nation, under God, shall have a new birth of freedom—and that government of the people, by the people, for the people, shall not perish from the earth."

His Gettysburg Address seemed to embody the Northern cause, but Lincoln's Union had not finished yet. By the end of 1862 he knew that the Union, even saved, would be changed. Lincoln understood power and the ways it grew. He understood, too, that the United States had the vitality both to fight and to grow. As historian James McPherson has said, the Union "to a remarkable degree, was able to produce both guns and butter." This would not have been so had Lincoln not encouraged revolutionary shifts in society, economy, and politics, which opened the way to world power.

He achieved a real and lasting revolution—a new and fairer land of freedom, a land of promise and good hope.

DAVIS'S SOUTHERN WAY OF WAR

On May 11, 1861, the Confederate Congress proclaimed that "war exists between the United States and the Confederate States." That laconic phrase announced far more than war: it declared a forever different future. At the moment he stood before the crowd in Montgomery to deliver his inaugural address, Jefferson Davis recognized the differentness of everything. No matter that Provisional Congressmen hewed to hands-off policies and boasted their conservatism, war meant new realities. Davis recognized immediately the shifts in executive patterns as he began the dual projects of making a country and fashioning a cause.

If Lincoln's problems in defining war aims were hard, Davis accepted the even stiffer challenge of forging a nation from disparate states and then articulating a cause worthy of it. As he groped toward a government able to govern, he groped, too, toward ways of national defense. Southern insistence on a defensive posture, on being left alone in independence, imposed limits on strategy. Although Davis knew that territorial protection might deny some important offensive options to the Confederacy, he also knew that in a country formed to sustain states' rights, localism had peculiar force.

Davis was a states' rights man; some said he was Calhoun's familiar once that gaunt defender of "the poor south" had gone, a man strong for secession and the wants of the minorities. No one else matched the Confederate chief executive in grasp of the tender honor of his countrymen; he knew their petulant independence, their quixotic devotion to the protocols of the *geste*. He knew them in the fullness of their romantic selves because he was one of them—and yet he was not. When he took his oath of office, he became a new man, a Confederate. He was a man who needed to be needed, and he would become the Confederacy's most needed man—much more than his country guessed.

Look at him clearly, at that chiseled face, those questing eyes, the tall figure leaning into something always—an etching out of life. Dignity he had, a determination to go with the strong chin and deep eyes, a dignity holding temper at bay though the temper showed at times in the impatience of being right. Lincoln attracted caricature, Davis only portraits in almost classic guise. Was there, in that odd difference, some mysterious contrast of attraction, some telltale clue

Jefferson Davis in wartime

to character? To his Northern enemies he could look ungainly and a kind of Rebel "King Linkum," but the doggerel and the cartoons yielded to a Southern schoolbook poem:

Jeff Davis rides a snow white horse,
Abe Lincoln rides a mule.
Jeff Davis is a gentleman,
Abe Lincoln is a fool.

Some observers of his early days in office wondered if his chill dignity might congeal a revolution. There were some, though, who looked behind aloofness to see a shy man's fiery soul.

Those who watched his early actions could see a nationalist in the making. Just as Lincoln pushed against the boundaries of things to make a country fit a war, so Davis stretched his vision beyond the borders of the states. He grew with the job. Aware of the need for quick Confederate sentiment, Davis worked to build a central government around which the Southern people could rally, and he built a firm foundation. Long a strict constructionist—a believer in the constitution as written—he saw that charter as a source of national power. Where others brandished the document to hold back centralism, he seized on it as "the supreme law of the land," as a source of executive authority. He worried about federal force and promised Confederates in his inaugural that it would be properly used. And he kept the promise, although some extreme states' righters carped about his push for strong government.

Using the war powers authority, Davis worked to build a national army from his first days in office; few Southerners appreciated the importance of that fact. A national army, raised by the congress, with only nominal nodding to the states, stood as the firmest prop of the central government. Although state troops were requested and received, they were absorbed into the national forces. And while officers were elected through regimental level, the Confederate government commissioned them and insisted on designating brigade, division, corps, and army commanders.

Continuing efforts to establish his own and his administration's authority, the president persuaded the Provisional Congress to assume charge of all military operations within Confederate borders, a deft thrust at state efforts to make war. Comfortable in martial matters because of his long service as secretary of war, Davis had no qualms about keeping the armies close to the presidency. A problem often

23

for the seven war secretaries who tried to serve him, this Davis foible had good and bad results.

Early organizational success owed much to his understanding of armies and soldiers; his ultimate design of an "offensive-defensive" strategy did much to conserve inferior Confederate strength for major battles and a long war. Triumphs of "Lee's Army," the Army of Northern Virginia, proceeded in part from the military and logistical policies devised by a president not wedded to precedent.

A few Confederate defeats rested on the president's persistent friendships. Some scholars argue that the Confederacy perished of states' rights—an almost equal case might be made for cronyism. Two blatant examples irked a lot of Confederates: the cases of Braxton Bragg and Lucius Bellinger Northrop. Bragg, a longtime friend with prominent family connections in North Carolina and across the South, seemed a paragon of martial mien—heavy brows dominated his angular face and accentuated piercing, restless eyes; salt and pepper hair and beard gave strength; an immaculate and well-filled uniform finished the warrior portrait. What could such a model soldier lack? He had all the tools for success save one: a fighting heart. Much like his enemy George McClellan, Bragg could fashion an army out of rabble and burnish it to the finest mettle, but then he would agonize about launching his creation against the foe. His Kentucky campaign lingered in Confederate minds as a kind of saga of lost lives and chances; Lookout Mountain and Missionary Ridge confirmed his opposite talents. As his career gathered wreckage, President Davis stuck to him, even elevated him at last to a kind of chief-of-staff position in Richmond.

At the same time, the president clung to his friend Northrop, the commissary general of the Confederate Army—a curmudgeon gifted in famine. As rations dwindled, as Confederate ranks shrank in size and strength, Northrop quibbled about procedure and attacked Southern generals who lost territory from which food might be taken. Even the gentlemanly Robert E. Lee detested Northrop and finally refused contact with him. Only near the end did the chief executive replace Northrop—too late to reverse starvation. These examples of cherished professional incompetence were seen by many as evidence of a presidential stubbornness ill afforded in a beleaguered nation. Other examples were cited, too, as the war lengthened and Davis's popularity waned.

There was another side to Davis's stubbornness, not of cronyism but of animus, a side that cost the Confederacy the best services of two gifted soldiers, Joseph E. Johnston and Pierre G. T. Beauregard. Johnston and Davis had a serious altercation early in their lives (some accounts suggest the rupture came during West Point days), which lingered in memory and dimmed the president's appreciation of a careful soldier with a mind of his own. A corrosive quarrel about Johnston's relative rank after promotion to full general refreshed animosity after the Battle of First Manassas (Bull Run), and although the president at one time gave Johnston what was potentially the most important command of the war, suspicion eroded Johnston's confidence, and he lost a magnificent opportunity. The president reluctantly put him in charge of the Army of Tennessee during the crucial 1864 summer campaign in Georgia. A superior Fabian retreat before Sherman finally placed Johnston's army in the Atlanta siege lines, and when the general refused to tell the president his plans, he was relieved and put on the shelf for agonizing months. A final fling at command, after Lee became general in chief of the Confederacy's armies, brought a small victory and final surrender to Sherman. Had the general and the president trusted each other, Johnston might have been among the most effective of Confederate army commanders.

Beauregard, too, might have been the Confederacy's best strategist. A mercurial soldier, the Great Creole had dash, quick emotion, and a flamboyance irritating to Davis's austerity. Early experience with Beauregard raised questions in the president's mind. Although he finally fought well at First Manassas, Beauregard's early battle plan wallowed in Byzantine confusion and he seemed almost adrift in ambiguities as he lined his men along Bull Run Creek. Saved by the arrival of Joseph E. Johnston's army, Beauregard got control of himself and won the battle. But Davis remembered the confusion and wondered. Sent to the west as second in command to Albert Sidney Johnston – a presidential favorite – Beauregard showed sound strategical sense but logistical imprecision. He wanted to do the right things but did not fully grasp his supply and transportation problems. A strange and sulking illness took him to a long rest and then assignment to Charleston's defense, where he did extremely well. A heroic defense of Petersburg showed again his battle sense, but appointment to a theater command without power took him from his best role. Davis never trusted this small man with the large ego, never let him have a chance to show the kind of strategical sense that might have coordinated Confederate operations. Instead of bringing Bragg to

Richmond in a chief-of-staff slot, Davis might have fared better with Beauregard. Personalities made that impossible—sadly for the Southern cause.

These instances make a hard case against Davis's personal and official judgment. They are, though, somewhat out of context. Davis surely had a difficult personality, did have a stubborn streak made large by his place and problems. But he had to work with whom and what he found available in his new land and make the best of it. If sometimes he erred, it is scarcely surprising—all presidents err. Most have tempers, and most rely on cronies. The crises crowding the Confederacy permitted Davis no luxury of temper, no leeway in mistakes —he had no margin of error. This meant, of course, that history denied him both humanity and success. Some scholars suggest that Davis lacked skill even in military matters and that his small-mindedness quenched Confederate successes in the field. This argument is unfair because it fixes only on victory as the basis of judgment. Fairest measure of the man would rest on how he built his cause and how he ran the war.

Since he knew Southerners well, he knew that the quick and fiery patriotism sweeping the Confederacy in early weeks would fade when quick victory did not come, fade into a disgruntled resentment of long privation. So he told his countrymen the wages of independence in public speeches in Richmond, before Congress, in his "swings around the Confederacy," and in encouraging clergymen to preach nationalistic sermons. In this modern propaganda effort, Davis tried to make "public war." His message ran fairly constant: a long war requires long devotion, steady sacrifice, the kind of doggedness that beat the English almost a hundred years before.

Davis taught by example. He worked long hours, gave exhausting devotion to administrative and legislative details, refused to yield to neuralgia and dyspepsia, took no leave from duty—and expected no less from any wartime patriot. All could see the results. A government came into being, an army of more than seventy thousand men by early April, 1861, a nation with belligerent rights conferred by Great Britain and France, a small but obvious navy.

From the beginning he offered a hard program to congress, one of strong taxation and increasingly tough war measures. Money lingered as the greatest need and neither Davis nor Secretary of the Treasury Christopher Memminger could devise a sound monetary policy. Memminger had conservative, hard-money plans to raise funds by taxes and borrowing, but, when these measures failed to produce enough, he was forced to issue inflationary paper currency. Some efforts were made – not serious enough – to use cotton as money abroad. Since England and France were textile producers and dependent on Southern cotton, it might well have created credit. Davis, Memminger, and gifted Secretary of State Judah P. Benjamin did succeed in negotiating a $15 million loan with Emile Erlanger & Co. of Paris in January, 1863. They could have had more, but congress feared to put a heavy debt burden on future generations! Congress often balked at Davis's war programs; its members chafed in the traces of necessity. But the president largely got his way, even in dark days of rising animosity against a Confederacy ever more in Yankee guise.

For those who feared a horrid Sparta rising from the ashes of states' rights, comfort could be taken in the way Jefferson Davis acknowledged civilian control of the war, from his refusal – unlike Lincoln – to use executive power in declaring martial law or suspending civil courts. When abrogation of habeas corpus became necessary in active war zones, Davis sought congressional approval. He did not always get it from a body devoted to law above emergency. Using the power carefully, Davis gave army commanders the right to detain disloyal people without resort to civil procedure and to suppress seditious activities. Although this power was curtailed and later withdrawn, Davis used suspension of the writ effectively to strengthen threatened areas.

In one arena he deliberately spared suspension – against the press. Lincoln often attacked seditious papers and journals. Davis's administration suffered bitter tirades from various newspapers, including some in Richmond, but did little more than protest through friendlier columns. Even in the direst straits, the South did not muzzle public opinion. Admirable as this policy is on the surface, it doubtless did encourage dissension and helped lower Confederate morale. Davis, like Lincoln, ought to have tried selective control of sedition to enhance centralization.

By the end of 1862 independence became the president's personal and official war aim. His main program for winning that goal was centralization of power, authority, and administration in the Confederate government. Centralization flew in the face of states' rights and consequently earned fierce protests from ardent secessionists like Gov. Joseph E. Brown of Georgia and Gov. Zebulon B. Vance of North Carolina. Nothing attacked local authority more directly than conscription. Davis, pushed by his new secretary of war (confirmed March 19, 1862), George W. Randolph, came to a vital decision about governmental authority and manpower. He urged, and finally persuaded, congress to pass the first draft law in American history on April 16, 1862, which made all white men between eighteen and thirty-five liable to military service. Class exemptions preserved essential civilian jobs, although excusing planters who owned twenty slaves or more brought cries of "a rich man's war and a poor man's fight."

To those who screamed about dictatorship the best answer was necessity. Confederate ranks faced decimation with expiration of the first year's enlistments; conscription doubtless saved the army. And conscription showed, too, how far the president would go to secure independence.

Because he was not only the president, but also commander in chief of the army and navy, he had the task of devising war strategy. In carrying out his offensive-defensive strategy, Davis came to advocate increasing control of transportation and of manufacturing, since an infant industry needed government help to survive and grow into an essential tool of war. He pushed, too, for regulation of blockade running to keep a foreign lifeline open. Against massive resentment, he supported the war department's program of impressing (commandeering) supplies and food for the armies.

This program bore fruit. By late 1862 a prominent English politician, William Gladstone, proclaimed that Davis had made a nation, and by mid-1863 Confederate armies were larger and better supplied than ever and Southerners were thinking like Confederates. Still, the countervailing urges of states' rights continued and sapped a central energy. While the president struggled for supremacy, some governors thought of seceding from his country. Decentralization of state efforts hacked at the Confederacy to produce a confused image of decentralized centralization at the heart of the South's war effort.

Davis recognized his own flight from Southern tradition, knew that the things he made himself advocate, urge, try to force into being were anathema to a people rooted in a myth of the noble individual. When, toward the end, he dared suggest limited emancipation of slaves in exchange for service in the army, an increasingly beleaguered president felt the outrage and the venom of a restive congress and a desperate people. In the ashes of their cause, Southerners turned on him as an engineer of evil change, a destroyer of the Southern way of life.

To some extent he was exactly that because he made himself into a Confederate, first and foremost. As that new man, he had a vision different from moonlight and magnolias, a vision of a Confederacy boasting more individualism than the North, a place of restrained progress where people mattered more than things—even blacks whose freedom would help sustain commercial agrarianism. He lacked Lincoln's gift of language to evoke the vision that smoldered in his soul, but he came at times to eloquence in talking of the cause he nearly won. He created a revolutionary state, and when his dream was lost and his country gone, he could take some consolation in knowing that important things were left behind.

Things were never the same with the South—not just because of utter defeat but because of changes wrung by revolution. Keeping up the fight forced many Southerners to do the things they hated, to become much like their enemies, as they tried to wage war in personal ways—but the war had its iron rules of wreckage that wasted certain graces from before. All of these impertinences had value for the future. New people inured to sacrifice, Southerners were no longer prisoners of the past. Although they looked back fondly, they were readier than they knew for what would come. If they were not the Confederates Davis hoped to make, they were stronger for what he did. As he changed himself and fashioned a revolution in the Confederate image, he did more than anyone else to shape the South for survival in a different world.

What follows is a short account of the two revolutions Lincoln and Davis made in waging the American Civil War.

CHAPTER TWO

Coming

What caused the Civil War is a question that puzzles and fascinates always, and answers are as numerous as questioners. North and South split over slavery, economic systems, and ways of life, over different ideas about democracy and freedom. It seemed by the election of 1860 that the United States had nearly ruptured already, so angry rang the words in congress and in the daily press. Some dread disease spread across the land, a disease that witched enemies from friends and thinned the ranks of loyalty.

Aggressive Northern pursuit of progress caused some of the problem. Burgeoning with money and people, the North rushed into the Industrial Age almost as a reward for good Yankee business sense. All sections of the nation except the agrarian South followed in pursuit of the power of wealth. The South had lagged woefully—in the traces of the plantation system, in the thrall of slavery, and shackled to the land. And the South nagged at Northern consciences.

Democracy, progress, the graces that come from money, all blessed the land of the free and the brave. But what about slavery? The "peculiar institution" persisted from colonial times and spread with the cotton kingdom. Slaves worked in gangs, in teams, and sometimes alongside their "masters" and were the labor source in the South. Because slaves were essential to the agrarian way, the South adapted a society around slavery. But the institution had more than economic impact for the South. Sociologists would say that slavery became a system of social control, an institution that "solved" the race equation in an agrarian land.

The institution piqued increasingly tender Northern sensibilities, and men and women of influence began to believe that black servitude denied the promise of the Declaration of Independence and even of the Constitution, although that document did contain provisions for slavery–provisions surely the hostage of final ratification by the original colonies. As so often happens, political consciences appealed to religion for support. Abolition societies sprang up in both North and South–with many below Mason and Dixon's line before 1831– and a fierce campaign of moral suasion sought to have Southerners free their slaves. Not a great proportion of them owned the 3 million slaves in the South. According to 1860 census figures, out of a total Southern population of 9,103,332, there were 385,000 slaveholders, but only some 45,000 of them met the planter-class definition: 20 or more slaves. Not many more than 2,000 owned enough land for 100 slaves. No more than a quarter of the family heads owned slaves at all; most of those who did owned fewer than 5 hands. But even small owners were, certainly in their own eyes, part of the elite planter class–the class that set the tone of Southern life. Yet, many of the elite were uneasy with their social order, and freeing slaves was not uncommon; in 1860 there were 132,760 "free Negroes" in the cotton area.

A tragedy of history broke that thin cord of reaction toward freedom. In 1831, Nat Turner, a Virginian, led an uprising of seven fellow slaves in Southampton County and killed nearly sixty whites, most of them women and children–and in some cases drank their blood. "Servile insurrection" ran a horrid prospect over the South, with wild images of rapes and fires and gory mutilation. Much more than Turner's pitiful cause died with him. Terror washed in the wake of the blood Turner spilled, and across the South a new hardness of heart tinged relations with blacks. Where free blacks had been acceptable in most states, they now were barely tolerated. By 1860, the trend ran against freeing slaves. Where abolition societies had grown in the South before Turner's insurrection, they withered now, and in their place came suspicion and uncertainty. What would freedom's course have been without Nat Turner?

Results were dismal enough. As abolition rhetoric rose, Southerners felt threatened, isolated, resentful, and they turned from guilt to pride in slavery. Politicians and pundits began to speak of slavery's "positive good" and point to plantation paternalism as superior to the sweat shop exploitation of Northern labor. More, some planters boasted the idyllic "Southern way of life," against the crass materialism they saw tarnishing existence north of the Mason-Dixon line. Definition of this concept lacked precision but certainly the Southern way of life included balmy climes, moonlight, magnolias and moss, and "darkies" singing on a plantation owned by a benevolent despot called "massa." That much wrong clouded this dream Southerners knew, but in the wash of invective flooding from the North, they lost grip on truth and refuged in wishes.

Pressure built unremittingly through the 1850s, until finally William Lloyd Garrison and his fellow abolitionists took charge of the campaign to free American slaves. Years of suasion, of threatened legislation, of fiery rhetoric having failed, Garrison and his followers shifted from guilt appeals to militancy. Northern states in growing numbers passed personal liberty laws, aimed at negating enforcement of the Fugitive Slave Act of 1850, one of the linchpins of the Great Compromise achieved that year to preserve a Union stretched on the rack of property rights. Citizens who watched slaves caught in the streets of Northern cities and shuffled roughly into the clutches of "slavecatchers," fought openly against the Fugitive Slave Act, and hence, the whole compromise. Equal protection of the laws seemed a sham across the South.

In general, though, the compromise brought relief across the nation. Inclusion of legislation clearly marking the path of slavery's western reach, while leaving acceptance or rejection of the institution to the people of newly forming territories, had sense and looked sound. But loud voices rose against the compromise in both sections. Attacking it as "vicious and wrong," Sen. William H. Seward noted a "higher law" above the Constitution, which morally banned slavery in western areas. His senatorial colleague from Mississippi, Jefferson Davis, attacked the compromise as a triumph of Northern domination.

For most Americans, the slavery "crisis" dulled with time. Certainly not condoning it, Northerners were, nonetheless, almost inured to the bondsman's fate. What could churn that old Northern current of freedom running deep in Northern blood? Drama. And it came in the form of an 1852 American novel, *Uncle Tom's Cabin,* written by Harriet Beecher Stowe. Vicious scenes of white cruelties to slaves, an emotional story of Eliza the slave escaping with her child, of lovable Uncle Tom being beaten to death, congealed old horrors in Northern psyches. Southern claims of lies and exaggerations went unnoticed in a frisson of freedom.

More and more an aggressive press accused the South of barbarism, and words took stance for facts. Throughout the rest of the 1850s, the crusade for freedom mounted. And, as "abolitionism" grew in the American conscience to be the focus of all reform, the South stood at bay.

Gradually through the nineteenth century, the cotton states had turned away from the future; their citizens looked backward toward a calmer, slower time. Boasting the gentility of planter life, cotton raisers were nonetheless entrepreneurs in the agricultural marketplace. They wanted the profits from their labors and resented a commercial system that intruded Northern brokers, or factors, as middlemen of money. "Direct trade" with the world ports of cotton became a cry of economic freedom and spurred several trade conferences in the South that focused on ways to cut out the Yankee trader. They all failed to open markets but did close minds. The Southern position could be rationalized easily: direct trade for a natural product, of course, was different from the money-grubbing activities of Yankee bankers and shopkeepers.

Intruding on the growing placidity of Southern self-hypnosis came Hinton R. Helper's book *The Impending Crisis of the South: How to Meet It* in 1857. In an uncommon attack on class structure, Helper, a North Carolinian, sought to persuade non-slaveholding whites of their domination by slaveholders. The white middle class he saw as the strength of both North and South; the plight of Southern non-slaveholding whites he described as a kind of economic bondage, a state in which yeomen middlemen were sacrificed to the cotton culturalists and planters, who cared only for wealth, comfort, and magnolias. Free white men, Helper argued, were the future. Without sympathy for blacks, he saw them as part of the problems facing non-slaveholding whites. Because of slaves, yeomen were in thrall to slavery.

An insurrection of these disenchanted was Helper's solution, a war to drive the slaves from the South. Nothing pleased the Republicans more than Helper's radical book. Many abridged copies were shipped into the heart of black Dixie, where they affrighted already alarmed Southern moderates. Hasty and strident Southern counterarguments stressed the alliance inherent among all Southern whites, with blacks as "mud sills," doing the dirty work. Even if some whites had no slaves, they were not as low as the blacks and should take comfort in the color of their own skin.

As Robert Leckie has said in his new book, *None Died in Vain* (1990), white supremacy "not only helped to postpone the Southern social revolution for another eight decades, it also helps to explain why so many of these victimized whites rallied with such gallantry and in such great numbers to the 'bonny blue flag'" (pp. 75–76). A common bond of status touched the South in crisis.

Politically, the slave issue had all but polarized government. Southern leaders counted on a balance of power in the U.S. Senate for protection against the rising pressure aimed at their institutions. As California entered the Union without slavery, these leaders sought ways to open new areas for Southern expansion. Great sections of the west, long known as the Great American Desert, were now seen as possible areas for cotton culture. When Democratic senator Stephen A. Douglas, of Illinois, sought to smooth the way of Nebraska into the Union and secure a rail route to the Pacific, he needed Southern support. The price for this help was repeal of the 1820 Missouri Compromise, which proclaimed all federal territory free of slavery north of the line thirty-six degrees, thirty minutes. Like many American statesmen, Douglas feared the mounting crisis over slavery, but in 1854 he finally pushed through the Kansas-Nebraska Bill, which prohibited slavery in Nebraska and permitted it in Kansas.

Such a storm rose as a result that a new political party appeared, a free-soil organization that coalesced in time into the Republican party. More than that, repeal of the Missouri Compromise fueled old suspicions in the North of "an aggressive slavocracy" plot to take over the government. Quickly splinter parties appeared, supporting native Americanism, anti- this and that, a collection of frenzied reactions to the unraveling of politics. The venerable Whig party sundered over Douglas's bill; members drifted into other camps and the Democratic party finally stood as the last national organization left. But Douglas's bill had dealt it a hard blow. The Little Giant, as he was called by admirers and critics in Illinois, hoped sometime to win the White House under his party's banner. With winds of such violence swirling the political climate, his future hung clouded in some doubt.

Everything got worse with bloodshed in Kansas, where rival factions fought. Douglas, thinking he might calm the slave issue by his original idea of popular sovereignty, proposed that settlers in unorganized territories could decide by majority vote whether they would permit slavery. Settlers with and without slaves poured into Kansas Territory. Local elections were often battles joined by friends of each side who came to Kansas just to vote and make trouble. Novel ways of supporting various prejudices surfaced. The New England Emigrant Aid Society, which sided with Free-Soilers, sent boxes of rifles disguised as Bibles – the famed "Beecher's Bibles," named after Henry Ward Beecher, New York minister and Harriet Beecher Stowe's brother.

"Bleeding Kansas" ran luridly in the national press, as a scandalous series of outrages flared. Kansas frayed tempers everywhere, even in congress; there in May, 1856, Sen. Charles Sumner of Massachusetts suffered a severe caning by Cong. Preston Brooks of South Carolina – perhaps the first skirmish in a coming conflict.

All these controversies seemed highlighted in the election of 1856. That year saw the strong performance of the Republicans, who nominated John C. Frémont, famed Pathfinder, for president. Trying to accommodate all urges, the party opposed slavery and claimed the western territories for whites. The Democrats won by running Pennsylvanian James Buchanan, portrayed as the South's friend. An analysis of the election shows Buchanan a minority president. He carried the slave states, save Maryland, but won less than fifty percent of the popular vote. Republicans did startlingly well in Northern cities.

Dogged by bad luck, Buchanan could find no solution to the Kansas embroglio. In the midst of these continuing troubles, the U.S. Supreme Court in 1857 handed down its famed Dred Scott decision. The president foolishly involved himself in the proceedings, and he suffered the consequences of a judicial opinion that not only spoke to the matter of blacks' not being citizens but also addressed the unconstitutionality of the Missouri Compromise line. Northerners saw the decision as entirely partisan, since the chief justice and four others of the majority were slave-staters. Southerners saw the decision as a kind of vindication.

As the troubled 1850s drew to a close, both sections looked at each other's stereotypes and saw evil. Finally, neither North nor South cared about what was going on in the other section. Prejudices were fully formed, and by election time in 1860 two belligerents stared in anger across American ballot boxes. Splintering of the Democratic party during the campaign wrecked the last national political organization and made way for the triumph of the sectional Republicans, led by Illinois lawyer Abraham Lincoln.

A Republican course to victory rested heavily on the party's standard-bearer. Fairly well known in Illinois political and legal circles, Lincoln had served in congress but lacked national status until his famous debates against Douglas during the senatorial campaign of 1858. Lincoln hewed a moderate line but injected enough moral outrage against slavery to charm a growing abolitionist following. He had some Southern racial notions but could not balance them against America's promise of freedom. And he adroitly hoisted Douglas on his own petard. Remarking often on Douglas's professed belief in popular sovereignty, Lincoln pressed the issue of whether or not the Little Giant thought the people of a territory could really exclude slavery from its limits before the adoption of a state constitution. Douglas said yes: it mattered not what the Dred Scott decision declared; slavery would be excluded if settlers refused to enact the police laws upon which the system rested. That answer kept Douglas's position but cost him many Southern votes. He won the senatorial election, but the Democratic party began to drift away from him.

In the swaying mists of feeling, many people of normal sense lost their way. William H. Seward, distinguished New York politico, spoke at Rochester on October 25, 1858. His usually persuasive toleration broke as he dwelt on the mounting confrontations between North and South. "Shall I tell you what this collision means?" he asked. "They who think that it is accidental, unnecessary, the work of interested or fanatical agitators . . . mistake the case altogether." It was, he prophesied, part of "an irrepressible conflict between opposing and enduring forces, and it means that the United States must and will, sooner or later, become either entirely a slave-holding nation, or entirely a free-labor nation" (quoted in Randall and Donald, *Civil War and Reconstruction,* p. 124). Republican Seward's "irrepressible conflict," teamed with Republican Lincoln's earlier assertion that "'a house divided against itself cannot stand;' I believe this government cannot endure, permanently half slave and half free," laid out a line of pending political battle clearly understood by a threatened cotton section.

Events in a small town on the Potomac gave sudden urgency to one of Thomas Jefferson's most dramatic laments for the nation. The arguments about the Missouri Compromise had rung a dread tocsin in his mind. "This momentous question," he said, "like a fire bell in the night, awakened and filled me with terror. I considered it at once the knell of the Union" (quoted in Roland, *American Iliad,* pp. 3–4). He felt that a "geographical line, coinciding with a marked principle, moral and political, once held up to the angry passions of men, will never be obliterated; and every new irritation will mark it deeper and deeper." He feared that the South, someday, would have to fight for itself.

John Brown had different worries. He heard voices of a kind that called him to set free the slaves. He answered these calls first in 1856 near Osawatomie, Kansas, where he and seven others (four, his sons) killed several slaveholding settlers. Escaped from that deed, this strange and driven man moved to Maryland with his sons and once more took up the sword of liberty. Helped by abolitionist friends in New England and New York, he collected men and arms near Harper's Ferry, Virginia. He had vague plans about freeing the slaves and setting up a free state somewhere in western Virginia or Maryland.

On the night of October 16, 1859, Brown and a small group of followers took some hostages, seized the arsenal, and made ready to expand their "insurrection." Reaction ran swiftly across Virginia and Maryland—shades of Nat Turner still darkened memories.

Militia units were called out by Gov. Henry A. Wise, and some federal troops under Col. Robert E. Lee were sent to help the state. This combined force stormed the "engine house," and the affair ended in death for several of Brown's followers and his own capture. The abortive raid echoed Jefferson's "fire bell," as Southerners reacted in fear and abolitionists demanded freedom for their providential hero.

All the country watched Brown's trial in northwestern Virginia's Charles Town. Indicted for treason and for conspiracy to commit murder, Brown was convicted, and on November 2, 1859, he was sentenced to be hanged a month later. Rectitude and shame greeted the decision. While most Northerners accepted it as the rule of law, abolitionists cited a "higher law" and ranted against the death of a crusader for the right of freedom. Charles Town seethed with rumors, plots, and threats during Brown's last month on earth. He had ended the trial with a peroration on his deeds (Commager, *Documents*, 361–62):

> I have, may it please the Court, a few words to say. In the first place, I deny everything but what I have all along admitted,–the design on my part to free the slaves. . . . That was all I intended. I never did intend murder, or treason, or the destruction of property, or to excite or incite slaves to rebellion, or to make insurrection.
>
> I have another objection; and that is, it is unjust that I should suffer such a penalty. Had I interfered in the manner which I admit, and which I admit has been fairly proved . . . had I so interfered in behalf of the rich, the powerful, the intelligent, the so-called great, or in behalf of any of their friends . . . and suffered and sacrificed what I have in this interference, it would have been all right; and every man in this court would have deemed it an act worthy of reward rather than punishment. This court acknowledges, as I suppose, the validity of the law of God. I see a book kissed here which I suppose to be the Bible, or at least the New Testament. That teaches me that all things whatsoever I would that men should do to me, I should do even so to them. It teaches me, further, to "remember them that are in bonds, as bound with them." I endeavored to act up to that instruction. I say, I am yet too young to understand that God is any respecter of persons. I believe that to have interfered as I have done–as I have always freely admitted I have done–in behalf of His despised poor, was not wrong, but right. Now, if it is deemed necessary that I should forfeit my life for the furtherance of the ends of justice, and mingle my blood further with the blood of my children and with the blood of millions in this slave country whose rights are disregarded by wicked, cruel, and unjust enactments,–I submit; so let it be done!
>
> Let me say one word further.
>
> I feel entirely satisfied with the treatment I have received on my trial. Considering all the circumstances, it has been more generous than I expected. . . . Let me say, also, a word in regard to the statements made by some of those connected with me. I hear it has been stated by some of them that I have induced them to join me. But the contrary is true. I do not say this to injure them, but as regretting their weakness. . . .

Lies and parables and wonders came from Brown's rhetorical cauldron; the speech had effects to match its marvels. He had intended to shed blood; he wanted to set up an insurrectionist state somewhere; and he did actively try to win adherents to his violent cause. But what he said had far less meaning than what people wanted to think he said. Abolitionists were thrilled, considered him a martyr beyond price, and wallowed in an orgasm of redemption. Many Southerners wanted Virginia's governor to pardon Brown, or reduce his sentence, or put him in an asylum; they saw his martyr's loom. Most abolitionists wanted him dead—cold clay proof of a soulless slavocracy.

During his prison month, Brown kept up a steady, encouraging correspondence with outside backers, and he met his fate with a hero's crowning modesty.

Of the hundreds who witnessed the hanging on that cold December day, one alone perhaps shared John Brown's fervency of soul. Watch the scene through the eyes of Maj. Thomas J. Jackson, professor of Natural Philosophy and Artillery Tactics at the Virginia Military Institute (quoted in my *Mighty Stonewall*, pp. 125–26).

> John Brown was hung to-day at about half-past eleven A.M. He behaved with unflinching firmness. The arrangements were well made and well executed under the direction of Colonel Smith. The gibbet was erected in a large field, southeast of the town. Brown rode on the head of his coffin from his prison to the place of execution. The coffin was of black walnut, enclosed in a box of poplar of the same shape as the coffin. He was dressed in a black frock-coat, black pantaloons, black vest, black slouch hat, white socks, and slippers of predominating red. There was nothing around his neck but his shirt collar. . . . Brown had his arms tied behind him, and ascended the scaffold with apparent cheerfulness. After reaching the top of the platform, he shook hands with several who were standing around him. The sheriff placed the rope around his neck, then threw a white cap over his head. . . . In this condition he stood for about ten minutes on the trapdoor, which was supported on one side by hinges and on the other (the south side) by a rope. . . . When the rope was cut by a single blow . . . Brown fell through about five inches. . . . With the fall his arms, below the elbows, flew up horizontally, his hands clinched; and his arms gradually fell, but by spasmodic motions. There was very little motion of his person for several moments, and soon the wind blew his lifeless body to and fro.

John Brown knew what he had done. He had seared the raw Southern nerve of "slave insurrection." Long histories of insurrections darkened Southern memories, from Haiti to Santo Domingo to Gabriel Prosser's and Denmark Vesey's risings to the literal blooddrinking of Nat Turner's violent days. Cold and vicious fear lingered, not to be eased by abolitionist rhetoric or by promises of constitutional fairness. This fear had greater impact than Northerners knew and did more to destabilize Southern minds than all the raucous fire-eaters.

And at the moment of Brown's hanging, bells tolled across the North, watch guns boomed last heartbeats of a hero. Crowds surged and cried and mourned. Ralph Waldo Emerson put it aptly when he said Brown was a saint to "make the gallows glorious like the cross." The rite of the scaffold would loom for years over battlefields for freedom.

Into these crucibles of conscience came the election of 1860. American national elections defy foreign comprehension. A normally rational nation seems suddenly to become a kind of parody of itself. Rallies, speeches, promises, pledges, accusations, lies, humor, bathos combine in a frenzy of history. Some elections are more portentous than others, and everyone knew that 1860 represented far more than a moment in the course of history. For one thing, there were more than the usual numbers of political conventions. Expectations were that the new and sectional Republicans would nominate their man, then the remaining national party, the Democrats, would nominate the Little Giant, who would win, and all would be relatively well. Too much turmoil eddied through the year and expected things were out of season.

Beginnings were as anticipated. The Republican state convention at Springfield, Illinois, brought Abraham Lincoln to prominence through the simple devices of fence rails and slogans—the "rail-splitter" and "Honest Abe." In Chicago, at the national convention, Lincoln benefited from shrewd floor management and from the drabness of his main opponent, William H. Seward. Lincoln gained the nomination on the third ballot, with former Democrat Hannibal Hamlin of Maine as the vice-presidential nominee.

To Charleston came the Democrats, Douglas full of confidence and backed by power. The platform seemed calculated not only to help him, but also to assuage some of the angers in the country. Careful on the slavery issue, the party's pledge was to stick by Supreme Court decisions; as for the Dred Scott case, a bland endorsement left nothing to argue about. And Douglas surely came to the convention as the most likely man to patch the crisis, if not to heal it.

But also came a group of Southern dissidents, unwilling to stand with the Little Giant on his doctrine that seemed a sellout to the

Yankees–popular sovereignty. In the elegant Institute Hall, discussions quickly polarized. Alabama's William Lowndes Yancey, quintessential fire-eater, rose on the first day to recite again the grievances of the South and tolled a list of guarantees the section needed to stick with the party–perhaps with the country. He asked things often sought before: formal federal protection of slavery in the territories, strict enforcement of the Fugitive Slave Act of 1850, and some kind of constitutional girding for Southern minority rights. The difference now was in the high heat of the demands for the "Alabama Platform," in the truculence of the Southern group and their obvious deaf ears to reason.

Shocked, caught off guard by the eddying depths of venom, Douglas and his followers tried to mend fences. Arguments and fulminations followed; at last, the convention rejected the Yancey proposal. Yancey, his face red, his compelling eyes afire, rose slowly from his seat and began to walk out of the convention. For a tense moment he seemed again the loner of 1848, when first he took those measured steps–but now, here and there, others rose to follow him, and when they were all gone, complete delegations of five Southern states and partial ones of two others took their stand with Yancey and with Alabama. The Charleston convention sundered; delegates adjourned to meet two months later in Baltimore after a cooling-off period.

No cooling happened. A new Southern Democratic party made an appearance, dedicated to defending the South's rights under the Constitution. Leaders of this new party bolted the Baltimore convention and held a rump meeting to consolidate their strength, with John C. Breckinridge, incumbent vice-president of the United States, as their standard-bearer. A group of die-hard hopefuls put together the Constitutional Union party, dedicated to holding the Union together under the hallowed document. They sought to rally Unionists everywhere under John Bell of Tennessee. With such splintering, serious talk of secession surfaced.

And such splintering, too, gave the election to the Republicans. Although a minority president in popular voting, Lincoln received 180 electoral votes to 123 for the three arrayed against him.

Lincoln's election ignited secession sentiment. Formerly moderate newspaper editors turned into "straight-outers" across most of the South as reason crumbled in an odd relief of fear. Even Jefferson Davis, Mississippi senator and important spokesman for the South

IDAHO TERRITORY

NEBRASKA TERRITORY

IOWA

•Omaha •Des Moi

COLORADO TERR.

•Denver

MISSOUR

KANSAS

Fort Leavenworth•
Lawrence• •Westport
MISSOURI RIVER
Jefferson City

•Spring
Wilson's ✕
Creek

PUBLIC LAND STRIP

•Santa Fe
✕ Glorieta Pass
Albuquerque •

INDIAN
TERRITORY

✕ Elkhorn Tave

ARKANSAS

FORT SMITH

Little Rock

✕ Valverde

NEW MEXICO TERR.

Arkadelp

Fort Worth•

Jefferson•
Marshall•   •Shrevepor
Tyler•   ○ LAKE BISTENE
✕
Mansfield

•El Paso

T E X A S

Alexandria •

LA.

BALCONES

FAULT

•Austin

Houston
•

SABINE R.
RED RI

•San Antonio

SABINE PASS
Galveston

MEXICO

N

RIO GRANDE

NUECES RIVER

Corpus•
Christi

Gulf

Matamoros • • Brownsville
• Bagdad

0   50 100   200   300

Miles

Barbara Long

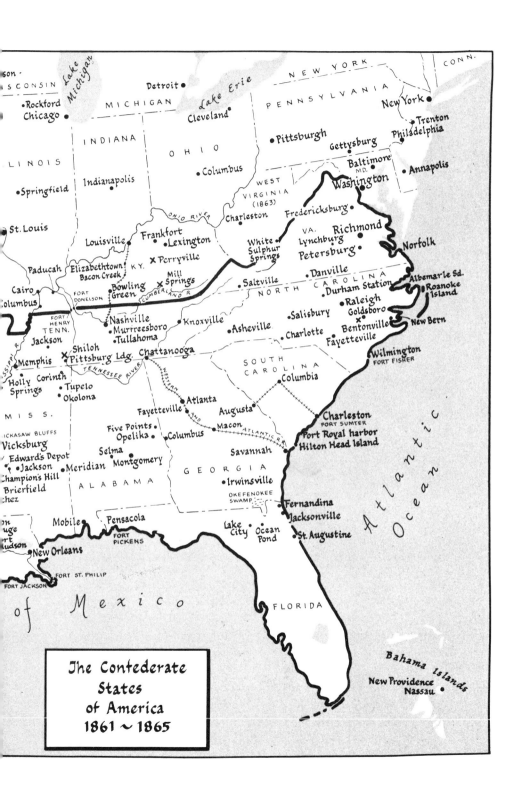

The Confederate
States
of America
1861 ~ 1865

in the Union, doffed his mediator's pose and pronounced doom if a Republican won the election. Why such reaction?

It must be remembered that Southerners saw Lincoln as the embodiment of "Black Republicanism," the spear-carrier of a party determined to end slavery in the South. His famous debates with Stephen A. Douglas seemed to confirm his antislavery views, and his studied ambiguity during the campaign, to justify the worst suspicions. South Carolina adopted an ordinance of secession on December 20, 1860. A combination of admiration for the Palmetto State's dedication and fear of the possible economic and social policies of Lincoln spurred secession conventions across the South. Mississippi seceded on the ninth of January, followed by Florida on the tenth, Alabama on the eleventh, Georgia on the nineteenth, and Louisiana on the twenty-sixth. After submitting secession to a vote, Texas withdrew from the Union on February 1, 1861.

As usually happens, moderates were crowded out by zealots. Secession had its own momentum and finished the fence sitters; many who doubted the wisdom of disunion went nonetheless with their native states. Most Unionists in the South shared the view that loyalty lay to the closest government (the state) and that the Union had second claim on patriotism. Some remained who urged "cooperation," which is to say they did not want their state to go it alone. Many of these were veterans of South Carolina's lonesome Nullification venture in the 1830s. Those straggling few who remained steadfast to the Union – such as Gov. Sam Houston of Texas – would soon be the "Tories" of the Southland and would suffer like their namesakes.

Leaders of the seceded states congregated at Montgomery, Alabama, on February 4, 1861, to form a government. Despite the wash of "independence" across the South, there was general agreement that a new confederation would have to be formed to face the Union, and there was general agreement, too, that the new government would have to be a good deal stronger than the one created under the Articles of Confederation.

Haste urged the Montgomery proceedings. Many who came there wanted to do the business of nation-making quickly, so that when Lincoln's inauguration happened the new president of the United States would confront a Southern government in being.

A majority of delegates to Montgomery were not fire-eaters, and a sense of moderation tinged their doings in convention. Most of the hotheads had lost out in the state conventions that picked the men for Montgomery. The men selected were, they thought, the legitimate inheritors of traditional strains of American political freedom; they wanted to show that the nation they were making came more in evolution than revolution. They adopted a provisional constitution that resembled the United States document in everything save the fact that the new congress would be unicameral, and they worked to perfect a permanent constitution that would be better than the United States model. Indeed, when drafted in a few days, it did show such wisdoms as the item veto and a six-year term for the president and vice-president.

Montgomery's delegates, too, decided on a name for their nation that conformed to conservative views of states' rights: the Confederate States of America. For national leaders, they selected Alexander H. Stephens of Georgia as vice-president and Jefferson Davis of Mississippi as president. Stephens, a well-known Unionist, dragged his feet toward secession and represented a lagging minority. Davis, a states' righter and defender of slavery, had taken a cautious stand on secession and quit his Senate seat in high hope and great fear for the Confederacy. For him, Southern patriotism had no limits—so he had a zealot's stout heart and short patience. He was, all things and competitors considered, the best man the South could call to fashion independence.

He knew far better than most fellow "Southrons" the fragility of his new country. Long political experience gave him perspective on the economic anomalies of an agrarian state in an industrializing world; experience as secretary of war in Pres. Franklin Pierce's administration gave him acute awareness of the Confederacy's military weaknesses. In his Inaugural Address on February 18, 1861, he would express the best hope for a collection of new "republics" flushed with the bravado of independence. He hoped for peaceful separation from the Union, but expected war—and tried to brace Southerners for a long and costly conflict.

As Abraham Lincoln stood on the Capitol's steps and gave his own inaugural on March 4, 1861, he shared some of Davis's qualms. His trip to Washington had been awkward. Detective Allan Pinkerton warned of Southern plotters everywhere, kept the president-elect's travel plans secret, and ushered him covertly into the capital near dawn on Saturday, February 24, 1861. Nine crowded days gave Lincoln a measure of the confusion facing the Union. A Peace Convention wrangled over proposals to save the United States, congress wrestled with various amendments—at least one of them to be "unamendable"—and waves of office seekers clotted in the Willard Hotel lobby for a word with the incoming president.

Lincoln had shuffled candidates for his cabinet, listened to varying views on how to save the country, and realized fully the reality of a crisis he had casually called "artificial." Everyone wondered what the mysterious Illinoisan would do; rumors preceded him, and they ran from admiration to derision. He had, since the election, kept quiet and ambiguous counsel. Washington saw a tall, plain, ungainly rustic—poor in political experience, rich in western jokes, and altogether out of place at a crossroads of history.

Impressions shifted after the inaugural. He did not, said Lincoln, have any intent to interfere with slavery where it existed, would not object to the proposed constitutional amendment forbidding federal interference, and supported enforcement of the Fugitive Slave Act. More, he assured Southerners he would be lenient in administering the government and would not put "obnoxious strangers" in the South to enforce the laws. The South, he argued, had no real grievances—differences could be settled by the next election. But the Union, he said, was "perpetual," and "the central idea of secession is the essence of anarchy."

Nor could the states physically separate—trade and political relations would continue. Would legal separation make anything easier? Let passions cool, he urged. "If the Almighty Ruler of nations, with his eternal truth and justice, be on your side of the North, or on yours of the South, that truth and that justice, will surely prevail by the judgment of this great tribunal of the American people."

Responsibility for trouble would be clear. "In *your* hands, my dissatisfied fellow countrymen, and not in *mine,* is the momentous issue of civil war. The government will not assail *you.* You can have no conflict, without being yourselves the aggressors. *You* have no oath registered in Heaven to destroy the government, while *I* shall have the most solemn one to 'preserve, protect and defend' it."

Memories caught some poetry in his heart as he spoke an emotional call for caution. "I am loath to close. We are not enemies, but friends. We must not be enemies. Though passion may have strained, it must not break our bonds of affection. The mystic chords of memory, streching [*sic*] from every battlefield and patriot grave, to every living heart and hearthstone, all over this broad land, will yet swell the chorus of the Union, when again touched, as surely they will be, by the better angels of our nature."

Lincoln's address rewards careful study. In this one speech, he proclaimed a policy of preserving the Union, focused on slavery as the evil in dispute, and fixed any war guilt on the South—not bad for a presidential neophyte. In addition, he had tried to put America's crisis in a rational frame of legal reference, put it in terms of political reason.

Reason, in this crisis time, ran differently as words played tricks in meaning and symbols stood for facts. Consequently, reaction to Lincoln's inaugural ran according to prejudice. To radicals, North and South, it sounded either too weak or too strong. Some border-state moderates liked it, and for a time the border stood firm. But many in the North found scant leadership in what they heard. To sober Southern readers, on the other hand, the inaugural came as a declaration of war. Although Lincoln might allow interruptions in local administration, he would keep the forts and other properties of the Union—a fact to negate Confederate sovereignty.

Both sides prepared for war. Rationally, the South had no chance in a war against the North. A close comparison of 1860 census statistics is chilling. *States:* North, twenty-three; South, eleven. *Population:* North, 22,000,000; South, 9,000,000, of whom 3,500,000 were slaves. *Cities (over 100,000 population):* North, eight; South, one (New Orleans), *(over 50,000 population):* North, seven; South, none. *Railroad mileage:* North, 22,000; South, 9,000. *Shipping tonnage* (June, 1860–June, 1861): North, 13,654,925; South, 737,901. *Horses:* North, 4,417,130; South, 1,698,328. *Mules:* North, 328,890; South, 800,663. *Industrial establishments:* North, 110,274, with 1,300,000 workers; South, 18,026, with 110,000 workers. *Annual Product:* North, $1,754,650,000; South, $145,350,000, and in 1861, the South could count only $27,000,000 in specie. *Agriculture:* Although the South boasted its cotton culture, the North had a large lead in the cash crops from improved farmland. The South led in cottage industry. *Arms production:* The South manufactured three percent of all arms produced in the United States.

In a counting of military manpower the South's chances looked grimmer still. The Confederacy had about 1,000,000 men ready for service in 1861; the North, about 3,500,000. Slaves were not expected to be used, save for personal service and labor, but slave numbers were important to both sides.

After the war, some critics would argue that Southern leaders ignored all the odds in a vain attempt for glory. Convenient as this charge is to believers in rationality, it ignores the importance of the cause of independence, the South's strategic position, and especially it ignores cotton and courage–two factors of value.

President Davis and his cabinet–men of greater substance than most accounts allow–agreed from the beginning that cotton would be the Confederacy's best fulcrum for success. Most of the industrial nations, particularly Great Britain and France, supported large textile industries that relied heavily on Southern cotton. Foreign recognition and intervention might come in direct response to the need for King Cotton. And although Davis and his advisers counted the odds against phantoms realistically, they did not ignore the rising tide of Rebel sentiment that spurred a new patriotic zeal. If, to cold calculators, courage eludes counting, it might be said that courage can arm minds and make strength in gallantry.

Lincoln followed his inaugural with a cautious attitude toward the two United States forts that had plagued Buchanan. One, Fort Sumter, a coastal work athwart Charleston Harbor, was held by a small U.S. garrison that had moved into the fort in December. The second, Fort Pickens, in Pensacola Harbor, had been garrisoned in January. Both were designed against sea attack. Suddenly they had awesome symbolic power, for they stood as Union anchors against secession tides–especially Fort Sumter. Southern authorities wanted it most of all because of its threat to international commerce and demanded its evacuation. Several members of Lincoln's cabinet thought Sumter too hard to hold, a risk beyond its worth. There might be a chance to trade off Sumter if Pickens were held. Lincoln groped toward a policy to uphold federal honor and reduce Southern fears.

Southern concern made these works useful tokens in an opening game of wits. Jefferson Davis sent three commissioners to treat with Lincoln's government about peaceful separation and about public property scattered across the Confederacy, especially the forts. Maneuvering to win Northern support for a war to coerce Southern loyalty, Lincoln cannily kept away from Davis's emissaries. He let his shrewd secretary of state, William H. Seward, deal with them in varying guises of cooperation.

Frustration tinged Confederate cabinet meetings as reports came of Seward's delaying tactics. Davis, though, began to learn that diplomacy can be a system of deceit. He came to suspect that the forts might be pawns in a game of pushing the South into firing the first shot. Aware of uncertain Northern opinion, Davis also knew that the Confederacy could not boast full independence unless at least Fort Sumter flew the new Rebel banner. How long could the South wait? On April 8, Seward told Davis's commissioners that the United States would defend its property only when attacked. That same day a messenger from Lincoln informed Gov. Francis Pickens of South Carolina that Fort Sumter would be resupplied, but reinforced only in case of resistance.

Rumors of a large relief expedition moving toward Charleston in early April caused serious war jitters. After anguished cabinet consultation, Davis authorized action. Secretary of War Leroy P. Walker telegraphed the Confederate commander in Charleston, Gen. P. G. T. Beauregard. Once Beauregard knew that Sumter would be resupplied, Walker instructed, "you will at once demand its evacuation, and if this is refused proceed, in such manner as you may determine, to reduce it." Beauregard worked to complete and garrison the works and batteries surrounding Fort Sumter. On the eleventh a small boat under a white flag took three men out to Sumter. They carried to fort commander Maj. Robert Anderson a message demanding evacuation. After long talks with his officers, Anderson refused, but said that he would be starved out in a few days. Beauregard reported this to Montgomery and was told that the Confederate government did not "desire needlessly to bombard Fort Sumter" and that, if Anderson would say when he would quit the work without a fight, "you are authorized thus to avoid the effusion of blood."

Anderson, informed of the new terms, replied that he would leave at noon on April 15 unless he received reinforcements or new orders. The Southern negotiators rejected this reply and announced that firing would begin in an hour. At 4:30 A.M., April 12, 1861, one of Beauregard's guns signaled the start of the Civil War.

Surrender of the fort on Sunday, April 14, triggered swift Northern reaction. Lincoln carefully crafted a call for 75,000 volunteers to put down insurrection. This call had the effect of a declaration of war and also fixed the nature of the conflict—Southerners had rebelled, hence their new "Confederacy" did not exist. Lincoln knew that Northerners might hesitate to coerce the South but would flock to save the Union. He also knew that the call for men would force some border state decisions. Lincoln hoped, too, that defining the coming conflict as a rebellion would prevent foreign recognition of the Confederacy—recognition would mean a Southern victory. Queen Victoria's proclamation of neutrality in May comforted Lincoln and Seward, but her concession of Confederate "belligerency" angered them—belligerency gave legality to Southern armies, ships, and commissions and was only one step short of full recognition.

Although technicalities tinged some border state withdrawals, Lincoln's April policy pushed Virginia out of the Union on April 17, Arkansas on May 6, Tennessee on May 7, North Carolina on May 20. Later critics would see Lincoln's proclamation of insurrection as a mistake, one that lost him the best chance to save the Union short of war.

While some border states' governors were rejecting the Union's call for men, Jefferson Davis issued a proclamation calling 100,000 men into Confederate service, and, when the Provisional Congress reconvened on April 29, he requested more money to prosecute the war and to organize the War and Navy departments.

By the time the U.S. Congress met in special session on July 4, nothing seemed the same. War had come, a war to run beyond all bounds of reckoning, beyond all previous American experience, a war to beggar all precedents. Small armies led by individual generals, operating in isolation, were gone forever. North and South edged toward the first war of the Industrial Revolution, a war to smash traditions and forge a new power in the world.

CHAPTER THREE

Beginning–The North

North and South began with the same ideas of war. The South, in building its forces, followed Federal military precedents. Both sides faced problems of handling vast numbers of recruits, of supplying, training, and organizing them into armies and, most urgently, of providing competent officers. Since the North had an army in being, it faced an apparently easy problem of expansion, while the South faced vexing issues of creating a national war machine from fragmented state efforts.

Northern military preparations were the responsibility of President Lincoln, but, because of inexperience, he might be expected to delegate most martial matters to Secretary of War Simon Cameron and to Navy Secretary Gideon Welles. Cameron, crafty Pennsylvania political maneuverer, quickly showed no art for war department bureaucracy. Truth be told, Lincoln could scarcely abide him, had appointed him with reluctance and in response to a nominating bargain made without prior approval. Vacillating, a slow decider, Cameron had every potential of adding confusion to red tape. Fortunately he had good professional officers heading the small national army of the Union. Welles of Connecticut, former Democrat, with big, dark brows accenting large eyes astride a prominent nose, had a puffy wig and luxuriant white whiskers that accented a querulous expression to match his mordant wit. Secretive, some called him, yet his diary told more of Lincoln's cabinet doings than even the daily gossipings of Washington. Of ships he had little more than common knowledge, but of people and their ways he knew much, and Lincoln liked his cheeky candor. His department boasted old ships and old sailors, but a tradition of adjustment.

Winningly unpretentious, Lincoln held few illusions about his qualifications to lead a wartime nation. Service in the Black Hawk War left him an uncertain militiaman and an even less secure commander-in-chief. But in the early years when he was teaching himself the rudiments of learning, he had made a close study of Euclid's geometry and of Blackstone's *Commentaries,* both of which honed a logic that gave him an uncommon basis for strategic thinking—something Lincoln came to recognize only with time.

Like most chief executives faced with war, Lincoln looked hopefully to professional military men. Fortunately for him, Gen. Winfield Scott, whose experience weighed against his age and lent wisdom to his portents, served as general in chief of the army. The army's senior general, hero of the Mexican War, veteran of the War of 1812, Scott had guided the destiny of a small United States army with considerable wisdom over the years. A dabble in politics as the Whig presidential candidate in 1852 exhausted that appetite, and he settled into honor as the nation's top soldier. Promotion to a brevet lieutenant generalcy—the first since Washington—in the 1850s crowned a distinguished career, but a niggling quarrel with Secretary of War Jefferson Davis over whether the secretary of war or the general actually commanded the army soured the venerable fighter, and he left the capital to sulk in New York—where he remained until Lincoln needed him closer at hand.

But the nub of Scott's argument with Secretary Davis lingered: who actually commanded the army? American military history revealed high command as one of democracy's unfinished issues. Under the constitution, the president served as commander-in-chief of the armed services. How did he exercise that authority? Did he issue orders directly to forces in the field? If so, why have a war department with a presiding secretary? What did that functionary do? Congress wrestled with command problems through the years. Off and on the office of commanding general of the army appeared in legislation, obviously with the idea that such an officer would serve as the president's liaison with the army, would probably issue orders for the chief executive, and would do such duties as might be done by a chief of staff. That often worked well. Winfield Scott had held that position since July 5, 1841, and had brought to his job quintessential experience and knowledge.

Lincoln had a mind to listen to this great, bulking hero. Could he plan a war to save the Union? Was he still flexible enough to see above the dull ruts of peace? At seventy-five, Scott apparently had lots of vision left, and he set about making ready for war. Grasping quickly that expanding existing offices, bureaus, army units, would be much harder than expected, Scott sought highly competent men to head various departments in the arcane organization of the secretary of war. These departments were hoary with age and privilege; their chiefs were satraps who presided over rather than commanded the quartermaster general's, chief of engineer's, commissary general's, chief signal officer's, chief of ordnance's, adjutant general's, surgeon general's and the inspector general's domains. Years had laced them all into changeless patterns of petty power–woe betide those who would intrude reality where even fancy fled.

Scott had no fears of dinosaurs and wanted younger men to rise above the regulations. Montgomery C. Meigs, the quartermaster general, stands an example in point. When he took office in June, 1861, he found an office wrapped in red tape and closely run by 13 clerks who tended their mysteries in ignorance of other supply agencies. Meigs, scrupulously honest, began expanding his force and by the end of the war managed no fewer than 600 employees. New hires would have to set a new tone of efficiency as well as honesty in a burgeoning people's conflict. Industry and business would have to move toward mass production as well as organize and centralize themselves in order to supply the war needs of the country. They did that with remarkable cohesion and success–so much so that by mid-1862 the United States could boast self-sufficiency in war materiel. The Union army became the most oversupplied war machine in history– a fact that caused Lincoln to lament the baggage clogging lines of communication.

This all happened because of a new kind of "American System," the vision of Henry Clay redivivus, embodied in legislation fostering land subsidies for railroads, a rising protective tariff, land for education, rapid advancement of public projects like railroad integration, and a new banking order. Bills tending in these Federalist directions had piled up in congress over the years, opposed always by a vigilant Southern lobby. Without that lobby to clutter progress, Republican congressional elements pushed a new order of prosperity and national power.

Railroads are probably the best example of government-business cooperation, with attendant expansion of influence and profits. Although the North counted far more miles of track at the beginning of the war than did the South, both sections shared certain operational deficiencies. Southern lines usually connected cotton-growing country to ports, hence were fragmented and resisted integration; so too with many Northern lines. While trunk connections were more numerous, small companies cherished their identities and shunned absorption by giants. This attitude shifted quickly, though, as profits came in the wake of cooperation. Then, too, the power to nationalize railroads given to Lincoln by congress encouraged railroad patriotism – and the president rarely had to use his power. These incentives made it easier for Northern rail men to work toward standardization of gauges – essential, since eleven different widths separated many of the lines!

Good things happened to the railroads as war continued. Government help in the form of land, financial subsidies, and high compensation for use of cars and locomotives (no fares were charged for troops) helped create one of the first really modern examples of industrial war. American railroads were the fulcrum of economic booming from the sixties through the rest of the century. If some argued against so much subsidy, against such an unregulated monstrosity choking out the little business, the vast majority of Northerners, caught up in a great war effort, were grateful for so strong a sinew of victory.

Profits were high. As Phillip S. Paludan shows in *"A People's Contest:" The Union and Civil War, 1861–1865* (1988), full utilization of the rails made it possible to pay debts and accumulate money for expansion. "Between 1863 and 1865," writes Paludan, "railroads . . . paid dividends of $28 million, $41.3 million, and $36.2 million." Interest to bondholders, for the same years, amounted, he says, to "$18.6 million, $19.1 million, and $23.5 million" (p. 141).

Railroad usage was refined by war's demands. Logistical lessons were more important than tactical ones; masses of men and supplies moved vast distances, these were the special legacies of the war. Some American officers, including General McClellan, had observed rail-

Railroads played an important role in the Civil War. This bridge of the Orange &
Alexandria Railroad was frequently destroyed and had here been rebuilt by the U.S.
Construction Corps.

road usage in Europe, but the fullness of mass needs eluded everyone. It remained for Gen. William T. Sherman to put the lesson in perspective, as he recalled emergencies of his Georgia campaign. What was remarkable in his memory was the fact that a "single stem of railroad, four hundred and seventy-three miles long, supplied an army of one hundred thousand men and thirty-five thousand animals for the period of one hundred and ninety-six days. . . ." Delivery of that much food and forage "would have required thirty-six thousand eight hundred wagons of six mules each, allowing each wagon to have hauled two tons twenty miles a day, a simple impossibility in roads such as then existed . . ." (*Memoirs of General W. T. Sherman,* p. 890).

In time the rails became the Union's main war artery, although water transport still served an essential role. The rate of growth of both cargoes and profit showed how railroads fitted into the scheme of a modern industrial state at war. Not many new miles of track were laid, but connecting links were the important ties and made way for the coming of transcontinental lines in the late 1860s.

Iron horses could not have sustained the Union's war and parallel expansion had other elements of Northern economy not worked in tandem. Paludan discusses the new Northern business climate in terms of the "second American system," and the analogy is apt. Banks grew in wealth and power as money came more easily with the greenbacks authorized in February, 1862. Hard-money men screamed about the debasing of the currency, prophesied ruination of the little man, skyrocketing inflation, erosion of savings, all the horrors of the Democratic faithful. Very few of these things happened because most of the costs of subduing the South were paid by such means as borrowing, excise levies, and raising the national debt.

Honesty became a problem in the whelm of military needs and orders to fill them. Secretary Cameron kept too casual an eye on purchasing and contracting, so bills escalated, quality control languished, and contractors became gleeful speculators on the growing martial corpus of the Union. Everything beggared precedent, which might work out well. In the meantime, waste would be justified by haste, or there would be no army. But someone would have to break the independence of the bureau heads and bring order out of administrative confusion. Clearly that someone would not be Cameron.

Confusion and waste in the war department and sloth among the Union's generals gave congressional Radicals a chance to meddle in the war. In December, 1861, congress created the Joint Committee on the Conduct of the War, comprising three senators and four representatives, ostensibly to help monitor honesty in supplying the war effort, but actually to push Radical objectives in turning the war into a crusade against slavery and Democratic slackers in congress and the military. Lincoln managed this committee with some finesse, but it took time and did mischief.

While cooperating with Lincoln and congress in efforts to restructure the logistical network of the Union army, General Scott addressed the toughest question facing the administration: Who would lead the Union's armies in what seemed likely to be a larger war than anyone had guessed?

There were going to be various geographical parts to the war, various sectors, and each would need its special leader. Western Virginia, a highly pro-Union section, Scott put under command of the younger Maj. Gen. George Brinton McClellan. Although he had been out of the army and highly successful in the railroad business, McClellan appeared to resume his military dash where he left it in the 1850s. Quickly he organized a force and waged an extremely effective campaign with a relatively small army, which preserved his area to the north and defeated scattered Confederate forces.

The question of questions remained: Who would command the main Union army, the army building around Washington for use against Virginia, against whatever force the Rebels put in the field? Scott, even Simon Cameron, wanted Col. Robert E. Lee for that spot. Scott, who had observed Lee closely in the Mexican War, openly considered him to be the best soldier he knew. Lee had been in Texas but came to Washington, and Frank Blair made him the command offer, with approval up and down the line. Lincoln had just authorized Lee's promotion to full colonel – obviously the president trusted Scott's judgment. Tempting the offer must have been. Lee, a judicious, skillful soldier whose career included several important commands and wide engineering experience, seemed almost everyone's best bet for success. Scott hoped the offer might keep Lee for the North – a coup that might weld others to the cause. The canny old general, a Virginian himself, recognized the odds and could hardly have been surprised at Lee's final decision. Lee deplored secession, would not support it; nor would he support a Northern campaign of Southern coercion. He would fight only in defense of Virginia. He declined the great opportunity.

Scott considered several other officers, in various department commands, as he looked for someone else to take charge of the large Federal army gathering near Washington, D.C. On May 28, 1861, Brig. Gen. (soon to be major general) Irwin McDowell received command of the major Federal army and of the Department of Northeastern Virginia, which included the troops mustering at Alexandria and in the Union capital. A competent professional, McDowell suffered the limitations of long service in a small American army. He quickly showed ability as an organizer.

As recruits clotted around Washington, McDowell and his staff struggled to use regulars to mold volunteers into soldiers, to fashion an army from an amalgam of enthusiasts. This difficult task was complicated by a growing national urge to attack the Rebels. President Lincoln, not yet a paragon of patience, also demanded action. McDowell, still learning his job and his army, wisely delayed advancing into Virginia until strength, training, and prudence allowed. Problems abounded. Not only did receiving and training men occupy every day, but also logistical tangles confused everything. The Eleventh Massachusetts Infantry had twenty-five wagons for the baggage of 950 men—the kind of ratio to appall Lincoln. Thousands of horses and mules had to be tended and distributed. Rifles, ammunition, cannon, wagons, harness, uniforms, shoes, all the stuff of armies had to be sorted, stored, inventoried, and issued. Field hospitals were new and untested, and doctors too few. Officers were usually as raw and untrained as their men. Everywhere McDowell looked, chaos roiled his camps.

Gradually came a kind of order. Streets could be seen amidst the sea of tents; men marched in semblance of formations; artillery batteries took shape; cavalry galloped without undue damage. Unlikely as it seemed, the Army of the Potomac came into being, a huge force of nearly 35,000 men. Most of these recruits were volunteers and they constituted a motley collection of hopefuls in uniform. Many were state troops, or recently such, showing the rawness of militia and often sporting different clothes and marks of rank. Various states offered various troops, and there was a lot of state pride on show as they mustered. True, the differences were not as bizarre as in Southern camps, but variegated militia looks bespoke states' rights alive in the Union army. Some units had city provenance—witness the Mozart Regiment from New York, a group of musicians proficient in strings and chords and soon in the tunes of glory. Witness, too, the 11th New York Fire Zouaves, a crack unit made up of men from the New

York Fire Department and proud of their colorful French-style baggy pantaloons, short coats, and fezzes.

Nobody had commanded so many before; what precedents there were existed in the pages of military manuals and more detailed works. Some students of war could point to Caesar's *Commentaries* as a good primer for organization. But Antoine Henri de Jomini, more than anyone else, set the formal pattern for the Civil War because of his classic book *The Art of War* (1838). Karl von Clausewitz came to be regarded as the great war teacher, after his important volume *On War* (1831) earned worldwide attention in the latter part of the nineteenth century. However, his work did not receive an English translation until 1873, and although most American officers liked to think they knew his work, fancy exceeded fact. And if many of them did not actually know Jomini, most of them had been exposed to some Jominian ideas through other works. Graduates of the United States Military Academy had absorbed Napoleonic history and theory through the classes and texts of Dennis Hart Mahan, who distilled his years of reflection in *Outpost* (1847). Mahan's enthusiasm for military history as a teacher of military art touched the mind of many cadets; one of them, Henry W. Halleck, beat his professor into print with *Elements of Military Art and Science* (1846), which seemed a kind of digest of Jomini's *Art of War.* Actually Halleck went further than the Swiss soldier who had served on Napoleon's staff and presented the first coherent argument for a program of educated professional officers to serve as a cadre around which to build a citizen army.

Jomini's pages were filled with almost mathematical examples of interior lines of communication, speed, concentration, key geographical points — all of which Napoleon grasped and used only when necessary. But from those examples, good minds could discern ways to turn theories into war.

Historians have been eager to offer the Civil War as a grand testing of Jominian, even Clausewitzian, ideas. It can be made to fit that mold, of course, but it came to do things of its own, to create new strategies, new ways of force, to be a new way of war. Jominian theory extolled the attack, even a frontal one, and some American readers like Dennis Hart Mahan disputed this idea before the war. Changes in weaponry — especially the coming of the rifled musket — might negate the charge, and the lack of training of American soldiers also pointed to the need for field fortification.

The influence of Jomini meant that French methods were important in American military thinking. Organization, logistical methods, as well as strategic concepts, showed French tinges as the United States army grew in the years following the War of 1812. Prussian methods, molded in the heavily theoretical *Kriegsakademie,* also tended toward true professionalism, but in ways different from the French.

From these different theories came the American concept of mobilization and use of large forces. Implicit in all these ideas, of course, were Napoleonic maxims of mass, concentration, and battle. These ideas permeated much martial thinking on both sides in 1861, and any look at forming armies showed Napoleonic precedent.

One martial dimension most manuals ignored: the lives of soldiers in camp and battle. Professionalism centered on discipline, on mathematical maneuverings, and on intricate chess moves made on remote and silent boards. Missed were the small terrors of living intimately with vermin, filth, battle, and death. Democratic armies are special cases, anyway, since they are largely collections of civilians turned temporary soldiers. Democracies have problems in handling and caring for citizen armies. Irvin McDowell came to fullest understanding of these problems. Managing the masses that clotted Washington taxed the ingenuity of neophyte provost marshals. Volunteers were unaccustomed to discipline, rustics resisted close tethering with a kind of good natured ignorance, and camp conditions worsened with numbers. No matter what the established services did to improve soldier's lives, much more needed doing.

Out of this early chaos several important volunteer organizations arose to bring home to the boys in blue. Tradition had it that the martial life reeked of gin and sin, that all soldiers suffered corruption. So, to Billy Yanks' camps—and to the Rebels'—ministers and Bibles came, and also, to Northern bivouacs, agents of the new Christian Commission. Sunday services were encouraged; against background choruses of "Stand Up, Stand Up for Jesus," Commission agents passed out Bibles, tracts, "knapsack books," religious newspapers, magazines, in a prodigious outpouring of voluntary money and zeal. By the end of the war the Christian Commission had raised $6 million for its missionary work (Paludan, *A People's Contest,* p. 354). Sharing the work of directly helping troops, another private organization, the United States Sanitary Commission, also raised millions. Its agents delivered fruit and vegetables and personal needs to the ranks, visited the wounded and sick in hospitals, served as scribes for letters home.

Combined with a variety of local societies also trying to help, these amazingly successful associations anticipated the United Service Organization of the Second World War and eased the burden of homesickness and camp life.

As McDowell's army took shape, efforts to assuage camp conditions were vital. Soldier effectiveness depended on morale – that much veterans understood, but the utter truth of it remained for battle proof. McDowell needed all the help he could get in mustering a useful force.

Lincoln had little knowledge of these things, but had a shrewd grasp of power. How could the U.S. army get at the Rebels? That was what he wanted McDowell to do quickly. The president pressed for action because further delay might cool Yankee ardor. A war without fighting could easily become a non-crisis. At a cabinet meeting on June 29, McDowell revealed his plan to attack Confederate positions at Manassas. At that meeting, General Scott proposed an expedition down the Mississippi to cut the Confederacy in two and make possible a squeezing operation around the coastal and interior borders of the eastern seceded states – his divide-and-conquer "Anaconda Plan." The cabinet and Lincoln decided to deal with the Virginia Rebels first.

Lincoln understood the need for a grand strategy, but political pressure – and inexperience – forced his eye toward the enemy capital. On July 16, McDowell's army opened the summer campaign of 1861 by moving west from the Potomac toward Centreville and Manassas in response to the rising cry of "On to Richmond." His columns were long, at first somewhat confused, and made scarcely six miles that first day. But he had advanced, and the North writhed in justifiable excitement because recent scattered military operations along the Potomac boundary of Virginia, in Missouri and Kentucky had gone the North's way. A few reverses in the far west could be glossed over in the wash of success.

Successes were also claimed in the South. As secession continued in the border areas and in some of the Indian Nations, national boundaries and resources expanded. Missouri's plight stood stark and clear during Saint Louis rioting and in the government's removal to the southwestern corner of the state. Much pro-Confederate sentiment persisted in Missouri. While sentiments in Kentucky and East Tennessee might be queasy, the Confederacy could boast that the critical

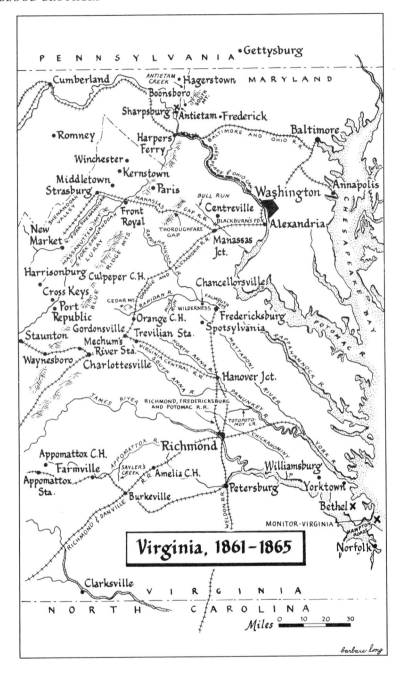

Virginia, 1861–1865

barbara long

62

border area clung still to the South. Lincoln's pressures on the upper South helped Davis's plans considerably, leading North Carolina and Virginia to join the cotton states.

In the weeks since Virginia had concluded a treaty of alliance with the Confederacy on April 25, 1861, sentiment had been building to prove to the Old Dominion that the new government would not ignore her exposed position. There were good reasons why this was true.

In terms of Southern power, Virginia could hardly be overestimated. Vital mines and minerals existed in the western reaches of the Old Dominion; the Shenandoah Valley always yielded bumper food crops; eastward across the Blue Ridge, prosperous Northern counties offered horses, fodder, and meat in plenty. Geography, too, gave special importance to Virginia. Her Northern border ran along the Potomac westward to the Ohio, which made river communications possible to the Mississippi country; Alexandria sat directly across from Washington as a suburb of the Yankee capital. Thrusting near the heart of the Union, the Old Dominion offered avenues of attack to either side. Virginia's location forced a good deal of Confederate strategy.

Richmond ranked as probably Virginia's greatest value to the Confederacy. Almost a city-state in the Athenian sense, Richmond stood apart from the rest of the state, most of which was rural, as a modern urban center. Down by the banks of the James, vast warehouses stored the commerce that flowed through Richmond. Close by were the black buildings of Joseph R. Anderson's famed Tredegar Iron Works, which stood as the only Southern factory able to make heavy cannon. Tredegar's great mills and shops did all kinds of foundry wonders: they cut nails, turned locomotive wheels, rolled iron and boiler plate.

In the James River itself sat Belle Isle, an important government arsenal. Richmond had long been a U.S. ordnance center. The Richmond Armory, a state facility, regularly received federal aid. It boasted little equipment but offered the compensating skills of master armorer James H. Burton, an Englishman with vast Northern experience, who had in his hands a set of plans for making Britain's splendid Enfield rifle.

Railroads nearly met in Richmond, but not quite. Separation of the two lines coming into the city showed starkly a major transportation problem. One terminus of the Richmond, Fredericksburg and Potomac Railroad sat near the heart of Richmond; across town, just far enough to make good money for the city's organized draymen, sat another terminus of the same line. A similar break interrupted the Virginia Central coming in from northwestern Virginia and heading south toward Petersburg. Differing gauges caused these logistical nightmares. Sadly, this anomaly plagued most Confederate railroads. Southern rail companies lacked incentives, or facilities, to pursue integration. Efforts by the Confederate secretary of war and the quartermaster general to promote cooperation and fair rates were only teasingly successful.

Southern cotton merchants, more than most Confederates, knew the peculiar nature of Dixie's rail lines. Everyone recognized that mileage lagged far behind the Northern routes, but the fact that many of the South's lines were short, unconnected, and designed to take bales from certain interior towns to ports was best understood by cotton marketers. The military implications of short lines certainly missed the general ken. Worse yet, almost no rail pulling machines existed in the Confederacy, and car repair and refitting shops were few and ill equipped for the wear and tear of war. Add to these factors the varied gauges that plagued the lines (Atlanta's five lines and gauges offer the best example), the scarcity of boiler plate and rolled iron, the increasing demands by government and business shippers, the South's shrinking borders, and the railroad situation could only be called nightmarish. A comprehensive plan of railroad usage would have done wonders, but congress and the administration shied from such outright socialism. Patriotism surely could be relied on to induce cooperation from all the lines; informal agreements with different companies were tried. Swamped with business from government and private sources, the railroads continued in quest of profits. Charles W. Ramsdell, in *Behind the Lines in the Southern Confederacy* (1944), concluded that railroad officials, "representing a multitude of small lines, were never able to coordinate their policies and services. . . ."

That unfortunate failure drove the Confederate congress to pass a secret act in May, 1863, empowering the war department to seize or manage railroads and regulate schedules and rolling stock in emergency cases. Not quite a carte blanche to nationalize the lines, the act did have teeth because it authorized the impressment of men, equipment, and management and most especially because it gave the secretary of war authority to detail men from the army to help cooperative rail companies. But congress could not move toward a comprehensive Confederate System like Henry Clay's American system. Confederate governmental power would remain fettered, internal improvements supported only in direst crises, and really tough taxes would come only in wake of financial chaos.

Still, for a time after the secret act's passage, train transportation showed some coherence, although problems continued to multiply. Secrecy itself worked against the act. The Confederate congress apparently was afraid that public knowledge would create public resentment, but secrecy enforced ignorance and weakened War Department power over the roads. Only in February, 1865, too late to matter, did congress virtually conscript the officers and employees of key railroads. Until then, timidity in the central administration and in congress kept energetic quartermaster officers from enforcing the 1863 act. Some of these efficient officials suggested coordinated schedules, pooling of freight cars, and other rationalization techniques—all were frustrated. So were almost all government efforts to build emergency, or "military," railroads.

All the sad future lay unseen in 1861. By most measurements, Richmond loomed as the most important Southern city. Many in the Confederate congress wanted to move the capital there; many argued against it. Richmond, like Virginia, lay exposed on two sides to enemy aggression. To move the seat of government there might overemphasize Virginia, to the embarrassment of the deeper South. Communications might be hard to sustain that far north. Those who favored the idea of a central location for the capital agreed Montgomery might be out of place and suggested, perhaps, Atlanta, as likelier to be safe from Yankee attack.

Richmond beckoned for too many reasons. Mary Chesnut, charming and witty diarist of Dixie, probably caught the best reason: "I think these uncomfortable hotels will move the Congress. Our statesmen love their ease. And it will be so hot here [Montgomery] in summer" (*A Diary from Dixie,* p. 51). Varina Davis, a realist of a special kind, is said to have responded that "the Yankees will make it hot for us, go where we will." As the Confederate capital shifted to Richmond, Virginia, on May 29, it signaled the addition of a lot more than territory or industrial strength. The ancient ambience of the Old Dominion gave special imprimatur to the reseated government.

Shifting the government moved the focus of the Confederacy and also the war. Virginia's exposed position demanded some Confederate commitment, and a switch of the national capital to Richmond confirmed that commitment. With the government came trainloads of recruits from the deeper South to pass through Richmond and muster near Manassas, some thirty miles southwest of Washington. Thousands of variously garbed and eager troops went through the new capital on the way to join the army commanded by the Hero of Fort Sumter, Brig. Gen. Pierre Gustave Toutant Beauregard. By early July, the Great Creole had about 22,000 men in his Confederate Army of the Potomac.

Intelligence had not been a fashionable part of military jargon in 1861, although the idea of intelligence permeated plans of all armies. Spying fitted the ideas of the times, and spying achieved high art. In the South, spying had a kind of family ambience to it, since gossip is the essence of a spy's business. Most of what happened in Washington could not be kept secret. Not only did newsmen snoop constantly, but also groups of Southern sympathizers did the same. Among the best ferreters of facts was a prominent Washington socialite, Rose Greenhow, who entertained lavishly and pumped her guests shamelessly. So she knew, almost to the minute, when McDowell's army moved toward Beauregard's positions. She signaled friends across the Potomac on the night of July 16 – McDowell was starting!

News of McDowell's advance brought a quick call for help to the army around Manassas. Westward, in the Valley of Virginia, Brig. Gen. Joseph E. Johnston – dapper, punctilious, "gamecock" of a soldier – with about 12,000 men had been holding the area near Harper's Ferry. Now he was ordered to move rapidly to aid Beauregard. In the first strategic use of railroads in the war, Johnston began to move his army on July 18, and his leading elements reached Manassas on July 19, in time for the approaching battle.

On the eighteenth McDowell's men had probed Beauregard's right flank and had become embroiled in unexpected action at Blackburn's Ford. They were repulsed, and that shifted McDowell's attention to the Confederate left. He prepared to throw some 13,000 men against the northwestern end of Beauregard's line early on the morning of July 21.

As it happened, that section of front would be lightly held, because Beauregard planned to attack McDowell's left at roughly the same time. Had both plans carried, the armies might well have switched positions! Johnston, the senior general, gracefully yielded command to Beauregard, who had been planning an action along Bull Run for some time. Beauregard's boldness came with Johnston's arrival. With some 35,000 Rebels on the field, an attack seemed feasible. The Battle of Bull Run or Manassas (the Federals named battles

Mrs. Rose Greenhow, imprisoned Confederate spy, with her daughter, 1861

after the nearest bodies of water; Confederates, after the nearest town or community) was about to start.

Beauregard's battle orders delayed the Southern attack and gave McDowell a head start. By mid-morning on the twenty-first, his flanking force struck a small Confederate brigade near Sudley Springs Ford and began to move eastward toward Beauregard's bunched legions. Unchecked, this advance would sweep up the whole Rebel line in a rolling defeat.

After Beauregard's grandiose plans went awry, he and Johnston devoted themselves to a defensive battle. They fed reinforcements to

67

their left, especially the Virginia brigade commanded by Brig. Gen. Thomas J. Jackson, late of the VMI faculty, as the main battle unfolded. While the thin Rebel flank guard grudgingly retreated in front of the Union attack, Jackson's Brigade anchored a growing Confederate force atop the Henry House Hill. Around 2:00 P.M., McDowell launched a heavy drive against the hill. As Confederates retired, Gen. Barnard E. Bee of South Carolina saw Jackson's line and rallied his retreating men with immortal last words: "There is Jackson standing like a stone wall. Let us determine to die here, and we will conquer. Follow me" (Vandiver, *Mighty Stonewall*, p. 161). Jackson's line did stand like a stone wall, and the whole Confederate line stiffened.

Repulsed, McDowell's men surged forward again and again. By 4:00 P.M. both sides were exhausted. A column of dust coming at the Rebel left flank caused considerable concern to Beauregard and Jackson. If the dust meant one more Union force, the tide would likely turn for the North; the Confederates were pretty much fought out. But a gust of wind unfurled a banner—the South's "Bonnie Blue Flag" of Jubal Early's brigade! Their right threatened, the Federals halted, withdrew, and finally stampeded toward Centreville.

As the rout gathered momentum, all kinds of flotsam were swept in its wake, including a group of Union congressmen and their ladies who had come out to watch the "Bull Run Races." Confederate cavalry nudged the retreaters, but confusion in gray ranks impeded proper pursuit. The victors were stunned by success, many survivors wandered over the field looking for comrades, some to rob the dead, others simply to bask in living. A great controversy would come from the failed pursuit—some critics damning Beauregard and Johnston for lack of zeal, others attacking President Davis, who reached the field late in the action. In fact the Southern cavalry was worn and scattered, wagons for captured equipment scarce; these factors, coupled with general fatigue, made an aggressive follow-up impossible.

Battle costs were high: Union losses amounted to some 2,800 killed, wounded, and captured; Confederate casualties came to about 1,900. And news of the battle meant differently in North and South.

Richmond basked in expected triumph, its citizens wrapped in winner's rectitude. Washington huddled in gloomy fear, Lincoln shocked by the disarmed and dispirited rabble that thronged the streets. These different reactions measured attitudes toward the prosecution of the war. Southerners were confirmed in confidence and knew that one Rebel soldier could whip ten Yankees. Northerners suddenly knew the seriousness of the war, the toughness of the Rebels. Bull Run brought renewed energy to the Northern war effort and gave President Lincoln the support he needed to press a hard war, a war to crush the Confederacy.

A dismal fact of war oppressed both sides – casualties. Deaths were expected in conflict, of course, but not on the Bull Run scale. Piteous hundreds of wounded clogged inadequate field hospitals; battlefield surgery lacked basic necessities and amputation became the solution to most arm and leg wounds. Hideous scenes and tales of field medicine translated for troops into a growing fear of being wounded. Families at home shared a growing resentment of inadequate care. So did Dorothea Dix, Clara Barton, and Mary Ann Bickerdyke on the Union side, and Ella King Newsom (the "Florence Nightingale of the Southern Army"), Sally L. Tomkins, and Phoebe Pember on the Southern. Dix served as superintendent of Union army nurses. Barton collected supplies and distributed them to wounded, finally became superintendent of nurses for the Army of the James, and was known to many who received her kindness as the Angel of the Battlefield. Years after the war she took a leading part in organizing the American Red Cross. Bickerdyke, a widow – middle-aged and determined – worked with the sanitary commission and became widely known as Mother Bickerdyke.

For the South, Newsom, a wealthy widow from Arkansas, gave herself and her money to setting up hospitals and aid stations across the western Confederacy. Tomkins, in early war days, set up and ran on her own a twenty-two bed infirmary in a house she rented in Richmond. Impressed with this service, Jefferson Davis made Tomkins a captain of cavalry, the only woman commissioned officer in the war. Pember, an energetic, winning widow, served as superintendent of a division in the gigantic Chimborazo Hospital in Richmond. Her war against waste, speculation, and indifference and her heroic struggle to save lives rank her among the best of wartime nurses.

Walt Whitman, too, served as a nurse in Northern hospitals, and the scenes seared the poetry in his soul. No verses spoke the scenery of the sick and wounded better than some of his war memoranda:

> These hospitals, so different from all others – these thousands, and tens and twenties of thousands of American young men, badly wounded, all sorts of wounds, operated on, pallid with diarrhoea, languishing, dying with fever, pneumonia . . . open a new world somehow to me, giving closer insights . . . than any yet, showing our humanity (I

Nurses with the Sanitary Commission often tended the wounded in field hospitals. This picture was taken near the Rappahannock River during the Wilderness campaign, in May, 1864.

sometimes put myself in fancy in the cot, with typhoid, or under the knife), tried by terrible, fearfullest tests, probed deepest, the living soul's, the body's tragedies, bursting the petty bonds of art.

Whitman grasped the growing cruelty of war.

Bruce Catton, eminent Civil War historian, observed in the 1960s that as the war ground on, it became for the Federals a war "against":

70

against slavery, against the Rebel army, against Rebel cities, and finally almost against the times. A kind of ineluctable process worked on the men of war, and hardness begat the same. Where there had been customs and forms and hopes for short conflict, time and disease and winnowing of comrades transformed the war into a revolution and turned soldiering to the business of vengeance. Across the lines, a similar shift occurred. Invasion and devastation of the South eroded humanity. Southern troops also took special umbrage at the use of black recruits in Union ranks. That seemed to incite servile insurrection, to mark the death of decency, and many Rebel soldiers saw the war after that as a crusade for survival against barbarism. These harsh changes might not have happened had Bull Run not been lost by the North.

Although things looked generally hopeful for the North, Lincoln wallowed in worry that first winter. Bull Run rankled yet, and, despite successes on the periphery, increasing numbers of Confederates still took the field, and more sacrifice would be needed to end an "insurrection" that had grown into one of history's big wars.

To those concerned with Northern war planning, it seemed clear that the conflict would be waged in four sectors: east, middle, west, and on the seas. Each seemed equally important, with special significance, in Lincoln's view, hinging on operations in and around northern Virginia. Yet many said the war would be decided along the Father of Waters, along that old river of commerce which seemed now to offer inroads of doom or opportunity to either side. What of Scott's Anaconda concept? According to that scheme, each sector offered opportunities to use the North's superiority in men and materiel to chop the Confederacy up, bit by bit. Not actively pushed by anyone now, Scott's plan seemed to be working itself out.

By the end of the year, the war's writ ran for the Union, but the future lay clouded in an endless mist of carnage.

CHAPTER FOUR

The South Responds

In the weeks after the Battle of Manassas, Jefferson Davis reorganized his army's command, appointing eight full generals on August 31; since the appointees took rank on different dates, jealousies were instant. That kind of pettiness, plus continuous Yankee incursions around Confederate coasts and borders disturbed a highly sensitive president.

Confederate morale sagged as Port Royal harbor in South Carolina fell, as Hilton Head passed to the Yankees, and especially when Roanoke Island—a kind of Sumter symbol—was lost in February, 1862. These losses, most particularly Roanoke, seemed the fruits of a piecemeal strategy, of weak leadership or indefensible stupidity, perhaps of strategical efforts that called presidential wisdom into question. Instead of concentrating smaller numbers of Confederate troops for the strategic offensive, Davis had scattered gray soldiers in a doomed attempt to hold the entire borderline of the Confederacy. There were not enough men to do this, as steady losses of important coastal areas proved.

Davis confessed his error but explained that weakness forced his hand. He pointed out to some correspondents that state governors were too locally minded for Confederate security. They screamed loudly that state defense came ahead of everything else, and their demands interfered with a coherent application of his national offensive-defensive strategy. Nonetheless, he pushed his plan throughout the war to better advantage than critics admit.

Dissatisfaction with the way the war was waged crowned a winter of bleak discovery—discovery of railroad weaknesses that compounded the rustic backwardness of highway development across the South; discovery of financial errors that robbed the South of monetary confidence; discovery of logistical problems almost beyond belief, problems made worse by the blockade of Southern ports that Lincoln announced on April 19, 1861, problems to beggar the wizardry of even a Lazare Carnot.

Rail inadequacies had melancholy overtones when seen in tandem with the woeful condition of Southern roads and highways. Transportation networks below the Mason-Dixon line comprised rivers, canals, and railroads; highway building had languished in an agricultural section averse to public improvements. Trunk roads were few; macadamized, or "metaled," roads scarcer still. Travel in the slave states had old-time connotations of rough stage coaches, bumpy buggies, worn horses, and shaken riders. Some cities boasted fairly good main streets, but beyond urban limits most roads shrank to traces and worse.

An agricultural section depended heavily on waterways for tapping interior locations. Would rivers and creeks help the Confederate war effort? Not nearly as much as hoped. Federal troops not only tried to occupy Southern ports, they also preyed on rivers and canals. Aided by a superior navy, they were able to patrol important waterways and to control them increasingly as the conflict continued. Union and Confederate marines contended against each other along some of the water avenues of war.

General mobility suffered, finally, from dwindling supplies of horses and mules. Although the South enjoyed a modest superiority in mule population over the North, it soon developed a horse shortage. Horses were used not only by the cavalry, but also by army artillery, field wagons, and ambulances. The navy, too, needed horses for all shore installations. Demand grew with expansion of military forces.

At the start, Southerners had no reason to doubt the adequacy of the horse population. After all, horsemanship was nearly every

Southerner's birthright. Virginia claimed some of the best horseflesh in the world, closely followed by Kentucky, Louisiana, and Tennessee. For that matter, every one of the Confederacy's states produced some horses. Parts of Kentucky and Tennessee soon were lost to the enemy, and their horse production markedly was reduced. Demand outpaced supply.

War overworked horses. Cavalry campaigns used animals in great numbers, and battle conditions put terrific strain on quartermasters to provide forage while also feeding troops. Naturally, military rations took precedence over grain and fodder on trains; when Confederate troops were undernourished, Confederate horses were veritable skeletons. In fact, the sad condition of Rebel mounts sometimes won grudging sympathy from Yankee soldiers, who marveled that Lee's wagons were kept moving by such pathetic bags of bones.

In early engagements, Southern horsemen clearly had the edge. By the middle of 1863 things had changed, and Northern cavalry no longer trailed along in the wake of spirited enemy horse. They were attacking, and their good, lithe western horses gave a stamina to overcome the old deficiencies in daring. After that, Confederate problems in sustaining the horse supply became pervasive, almost endemic. Again, Charles Ramsdell best explains the problem of horse scarcity as an important factor in Confederate decline. In "General Robert E. Lee's Horse Supply, 1862–1865," he shows that emaciation of the animals always was most severe in areas of active fighting, areas where opposing armies foraged widely and stripped the country of fodder as well as food. Reliance on horseflesh increased with the decline of railroad capacity; that reliance emphasized the crisis caused by losing horse-producing territory.

An interesting anomaly confused the Southern horse situation: Confederate cavalrymen owned their horses and were given a monthly allowance for rent and upkeep—an arrangement that largely continued throughout the war. Private ownership inhibited the best care for the animals, because individuals did not have the requisitioning power the military did. In practice, however, quartermasters often fudged and treated cavalry mounts as public property by providing forage and grain when available. Late in the war, horses were provided for cavalrymen dismounted in battle.

Wagon production was linked to the horse supply. Wagon manufacturing flourished as more than a cottage industry across most of the Confederacy, but large factories were lacking. Local production

Destroyed Confederate caisson wagons and dead horses – part of the growing short-ages in the South. This picture was made on Marye's Heights, May 3, 1863.

kept up with planters' and farmers' needs but could not support all of war necessities. Even had it been equal to the task, other shortages worked against success. Wagon production depended, for example, on manpower, on iron for tires, leather for harness, and on dressed lumber for beds and tongues.

Backward transportation strained Confederate logistics at the tenderest points of procurement, collection, and distribution. None in the Confederate hierarchy grasped the impact of the transportation crisis more clearly than the chiefs of supply bureaus. They all recognized that paralysis would follow in the wake of immobility; their efforts to find supplies within shrinking boundaries, to expand and modernize a nascent industrial base, to locate talented people who could find and develop dormant natural resources all were infinitely burdened by unpredictable conveyance. In ideal conditions, officers responsible for sustaining the armies would help in finding material, or help contract for it, locate places to collect it, and arrange distribution to the field armies. Even logistical neophytes understood the theory of centralized distribution—procuring army needs and funneling them to central distribution centers, such as Richmond or Atlanta, whence they would be categorized and sent to army railheads. Good as this sounded, reality negated it. Transport weaknesses forced Confederate supply men to spread procurement out, to find multiple collection points and sustain the armies from many depots close to the forces or close to usable transport.

Procurement faced staggering obstacles, beyond the obvious limitations of money. Munitions manufacture was restricted to some large arsenals and private factories, plus some small plants scattered around the South. But foundries capable of turning out cannon were all too few; private works were swamped with public and private orders. Private contracts brought in much more money than working for the government, and so private industry generally lagged in producing quantities of small arms and ammunition. Quality usually languished.

The chief of ordnance, Col. (later brigadier general) Josiah Gorgas, worked managerial miracles by creating government factories to provide artillery and munitions for troops throughout the war. He appointed brilliant men to various arsenals and armories—he made John W. Mallett, chemist and member of the Royal Society of Great Britain, superintendent of laboratories—supported experimentation with new weapons, and constantly encouraged departmental blockade-running efforts. Domestic production Gorgas thought the mainstay of his bureau, and he led the way in building governmental armories and arsenals, in helping such leading scientists as Joseph Le Conte create laboratories and small works, in helping Col. George W. Rains build a powder works in Augusta, Georgia, which rivaled the famed Waltham Abbey plant in England. His devotion to building his own establishments and his continuing concern for decentralized procurement and distribution pointed the way for other agencies and helped make the Confederacy a small but important industrial nation by mid-1863.

Realizing that saltpeter, copper, lead, and other minerals were es-

Brig. Gen. Josiah Gorgas, chief of Confederate ordnance

sential to munitions making, Gorgas created the Nitre and Mining
Corps in 1862. When its activities grew, he successfully urged creation
of a separate bureau, one that provided enough nitre and copper till
the end of the war.

Pennsylvanian Gorgas probably did as much as anyone—perhaps
more—to sustain the Confederate cause. By the end of 1863, the Con-

77

federacy produced enough arms and munitions to support the armies.

Lucius B. Northrop, who presided over the commissary department, became increasingly unpopular as rations grew short and starvation stalked Rebel ranks. Friendship with Jefferson Davis did not protect Northrop from a growing outcry for his removal. Although it is hard to see any mitigating virtues in Northrop's miserly record, it ought to be said that he tried some things beyond routine, that innovations were not unknown in the commissary business. Consider, for example, the Produce Loan, under which planters and farmers might pledge unharvested produce as security for bonds issued in 1861 and subsequent years. Initially popular, the Produce Loan confused treasury field agents and finally alienated producers, who feared they would be hurt by low prices. Non-agriculturists correctly considered this loan discriminatory. The loan did bring in some essential food for the armies, though; without it, it is hard to see how the field forces could have been fed through 1863.

The same must be said for Northrop's support of the administration's program encouraging domestic production of foodstuffs to the exclusion of cotton. As a part of Davis's foreign policy initiative of denying cotton to England, France, and other textile-producing nations, this self-imposed rationing did much to sustain food production after the fall of Kentucky, Tennessee, and the exposed parts of the Confederate interior.

When Northrop gave way to Isaac M. St. John in February, 1865, the commissary system had decayed too far for revival. Finally, in the siege of Petersburg, Lee's men finally existed on a handful of parched corn and a spoonful of sugar a day; armies in areas of greater abundance fared better, but never well enough.

The Confederate quartermaster department, most well-known of supply agencies, endured a good deal of public help. Davis appointed Col. Abraham C. Myers the first quartermaster general. A South Carolinian and West Pointer, Myers's solid army career seemed to fit him for a demanding administrative command. At fifty, he had confidence, knew army routine, and enjoyed a fine reputation. If any question tinged his appointment, it centered on whether a long life in routine, cloaked in the comfort of quartermaster regulations, prepared him for a conjurer's conniving.

Myers's responsibilities included clothing, sheltering, moving, housing men and animals, paying troops, and supplying post, camp, and garrison equipment—tents, tools (some for engineers), mess gear.

These duties filled more time than allowed. Myers followed Gorgas's lead and tried to find good men to put in various parts of the Confederacy. Clothing factories were established to extend contract procurement; small shops were encouraged, along with extensive blockade-running efforts. Shoes continued a sore trial to troops.

The department tried various substitutes for scarce leather—even offering canvas-topped brogans with wooden soles that pleased everyone but the infantry. With leather a pervasive need in the country, Myers's men tried to supply it by working with the commissary department to encourage creation of tanning yards. They even copied the ordnance department's ingenious use of several layers of cotton cloth, soaked in linseed oil, as machine belting. As territory dwindled and cattle, horses, and mules grew scarcer, leather joined the list of critical war needs.

Transportation stood the quartermaster department's main concern from the earliest days and became the bane of its activities. Myers tried creating a railroad bureau, put good men in charge, only to have them fail or leave in frustration. He worked to win help from the private companies; he supported a program to subsidize rail shops and facilities; he followed war department policy in delegating men from the armies where needed. Success eluded all these efforts.

Nothing brought quartermasters to more irritated notice than the chronic pay shortages that dogged the armies and government offices. Army commanders raised loud complaints about soldiers' pay; bureau heads joined the plaints and said that slow pay alienated contractors and talented people. Payment for impressed goods raised much of the ruckus. When quartermaster officers impressed private property for the armies—a practice legitimized by the Confederate congress's Act to Regulate Impressments in March, 1863—they gave certificates of impressment, which were presumably redeemable at the nearest quartermaster office. Aside from the fact that these offices were often remote, they usually had no funds to cover the promissory notes of the government—which caused loud outcries against the president, the government, and the war.

Old regulations wrapped in red tape caused some of the problem, and Myers, himself a red-tape product, tried to make improvements. But the real cause lay in slow appropriations and in the hectic history of Confederate money. The treasury department had much to do with the pay issue but managed to avoid most of the censure, although Davis did attack bureaucratic sloth.

By the end of his tenure in 1863, Myers could boast a rickety quartermaster system in decaying condition. He became a sacrifice to a growing war between congress and the chief executive and yielded office to Brig. Gen. Alexander R. Lawton, whose performance would rank scarcely better. Neither really organized the department; they improved production and importation but did not solve the transportation and distribution puzzles.

At the end of war's first year, though, the logistical bureau most exposed to public wrath was the medical department. Inundated by unexpected numbers of battle casualties and camp sick, the department struggled with a shortage of doctors—many of whom were "contract" surgeons with questionable qualifications—and with hospitals hastily sited, poorly staffed, and woefully supplied with medicines and instruments. Nurses were volunteers, many of them good, many indifferent. The plaints of pain and despond coming from frontline surgeries underscored the high rates of gangrene and amputation that were the worst wages of war.

Although the maimed and wounded did not know it, the South enjoyed the services of an original surgeon general in Samuel Preston Moore. A healer in the best sense, Moore worked tirelessly to make Confederate doctors truly professional, to build and support hospitals instead of depots for the dying, and to find usable medicine from home nostrums, Southern flora and fauna, and Indian remedies. Under his eye the 8,000-bed Chimborazo Hospital grew on one of Richmond's hills into probably the Confederacy's best, as well as the largest military infirmary on the American continent. Medicines were produced in government installations and in small, cottage quantities wherever possible.

Like his friend Gorgas, Moore urgently pushed blockade running. He successfully argued with Davis—who feared that official blockade running would confess the existence of the Yankee cordon—that the medical department had too few domestic resources and must depend heavily on imports. Moore and his doctors brought in more stores and necessities than any other supply agency save ordnance. Part of the reason for importing successes stemmed from joint participation by ordnance and medical agents in organizing foreign purchasing.

But as 1862 approached, the medical department faced an uncertain future. Still, at that juncture portent seemed good for continued support of the armies, if not for military operations.

In Richmond, congress took fright at military disasters such as Roanoke Island and queried the president about how much more of men, money, army, and munitions he thought would be needed. Quick to grasp an important chance to lay out the wages of war, Davis asked his cabinet for estimates and then compiled a wish list for 1862: 300,000 more men, an additional 750,000 small arms, 5,000 guns, 5,000 tons of powder, fifty ironclads, and a special fleet of "most formidable war vessels" for sea duty (Emory M. Thomas, *The Confederate Nation,* p. 134). Davis tacked on to his list a bitter disclaimer—no amount of money or legislation could produce these needs. Arms and munitions, as well as other war supplies in such quantities, were simply not to be had within Confederate boundaries or abroad.

So severe were the feelings of winter that some Confederates wondered if their country would know another Christmas—especially as the blockade tightened and staples as well as luxuries grew scarce. It loomed a good question.

CHAPTER FIVE

The Naval Alternative

Abraham Lincoln's proclaimed blockade of the Southern coasts on April 19, 1861, looked good on paper and nowhere else. The United States Navy had only forty-two ships in commission, and many of those were in repair. Numbers of the warships were flung far around the globe. Lincoln expected more diplomatic than commercial results from his announced policy. Although the Declaration of Paris of 1850 held that blockades had to be effective to be honored, Lincoln had some hope that Britain and European nations might find it advantageous to respect his paper interdiction of the Confederacy. He was right. Great Britain, whose concern with maritime rights had helped cause the War of 1812, chose to honor the blockade. When Queen Victoria proclaimed neutrality soon after Lincoln's call for volunteers, she also enjoined her subjects not to defy the blockade. Many did, but the precedent had been set. There might come a time when Albion herself would want a paper cordon acknowledged by the Yankees.

Davis and his secretary of state, Robert Toombs—expecting support from signatories to the Declaration of Paris—took pains to compile statistics on the sieve-like nature of the blockade in the first months of application. True, but irrelevant. Beyond that, the Confederate government strove to create a navy strong enough to keep the harbors open to the world's cotton trade. King Cotton would change everything, Davis believed. A shortage in British and European mills would force not only foreign recognition but also foreign help in mocking Lincoln's empty prohibition.

Both sides raced to build a fleet. Although small, the mere existence of the Union navy carried great advantages. Dry docks and shipyards existed on the east coast, which suggested a possibly easy conversion from commercial vessels to warships. Naval stores abounded in both countries, but skilled builders clustered north of Mason and Dixon's line. More than that, facilities for making marine engines capable of propelling giant wooden warships, or perhaps the heavy new ironclads, really existed only in the North. Even with these advantages, and with a rich industrial base, the possible effectiveness of the Union's navy depended on the skill and drive of its leaders.

President Lincoln selected Gideon Welles to be secretary of the Union navy. A more unlikely appointment could hardly have been fantasized. Ex-Democrat, New England newspaper publisher, Welles had a doleful man's acerbic tongue and a wig to magnify his cool, sardonic expression. To his office, Welles brought surprising ability and zeal. To cabinet meetings, he brought a captiousness reflected in the biting wit of his diary. About ships and sailors he had little knowledge, perhaps less interest, but Lincoln saw in his "Father Neptune" a fine organizer and administrator, who might learn. His challenges were fearsome, but he learned.

First among problems came the blockade, of course, and how to enforce it. With over 3,500 miles of insurrectionary coastline to cover, the Union navy needed massive help. Welles ordered a blockade semblance immediately, and the steam frigate *Minnesota* and the sail frigate *Cumberland* anchored at Hampton Roads, which would become the main base for the North Atlantic Blockading Squadron. Only these two ships patroled North Carolina waters in May, 1861. But Lincoln's navy secretary, aware that the president was willing to have the blockade strangle the Confederacy if necessary, rushed a naval acquisition program that emphasized not only construction, but also purchase of all potentially useful vessels—from sailboats to tugs—and pushed production of naval ordnance. Slowly the Union ship inventory grew, and more vessels deployed along the Atlantic seaboard. Welles went further. Major construction of big ships of the line received atten-

Gideon Welles, secretary of the Federal navy

tion, and unusual orders were entered for some of the new ironclads already used in foreign navies. Recruiting, too, received attention from the top.

Numerous rivers offered various routes to the Confederate interior. Quickly Welles and senior naval officers grasped the new tactics of sea-land cooperation in attacking Southern coastal areas, and specially designed gunboats were ordered to expand that effort. Marines usually participated, as amphibious operations became one of the most important, and successful, efforts of the Union navy.

With so much of the southern Atlantic coast protected by inland waterways, Confederate shipping, including potential runners of the nascent blockade, could sail inside the barrier islands until a clear inlet was found. A quick rush out would foil blockaders sitting around major harbors. Navy-army cooperation brought three important Union victories: the closure of Hatteras Inlet on August 29, 1861, the capture of Roanoke Island on February 8, 1862, and the signal victory at New Orleans in April, 1862. These joint efforts not only foreclosed many options for the Rebels, but also provided fine bases for blockading squadron operations. Similar cooperative efforts greatly helped Grant's Tennessee and Vicksburg campaigns. Indeed, without the ironclad gunboats bombarding Confederate fortifications, army efforts to take Forts Henry and Donelson or to storm Vicksburg would have been much costlier, if successful at all.

Experience tightened and improved all navy enterprises, particularly anti-blockade activity. As more ships cruised the Southern coasts, Confederate efforts to break the cordon intensified. Skillfully designed blockade-runners—small, speedy, light-draught vessels, painted to blend with the sea—plied the trade and were attacked by new, or updated, gunboats and cruisers. Lincoln and Welles understood the importance of shutting off foreign supplies to the beleaguered South. Blockade-runners were never entirely stopped, but gradually trade slackened to a point of diminishing returns. When Fort Fisher, the formidable work guarding the entrance to Cape Fear River and hence to Wilmington, North Carolina, fell to amphibious attack on February 15, 1865, the Confederacy's last Atlantic port closed. Officers and men on blockading service wallowed in the troughs of boredom. Weeks of uninterrupted sea duty, sometimes moving, sometimes not, galled the hottest patriots. Mails were scarce, food monotonous; men were cold in winter, stifled on summer station, and there were no girls. "Adventure! Bah!" complained one frustrated buccaneer, "the blockade is the wrong place for it."

Boredom might be relieved by capturing a blockade-runner and sharing the prize money. Boredom could be totally conquered in the derring-do of such officers as Commander Charles Wilkes, whose capture of two Confederate diplomatic commissioners from the British Royal Mail steamer *Trent* almost caused a war with England in No-

Captured Confederate blockade-runner. This 900-ton side-wheel steamer, with telescoping stacks, was rechristened the *Fort Donelson* after being captured by the Federal navy.

vember, 1861. Reckless and finally humiliating to the United States, Wilkes's "*Trent* affair" caught Northern enthusiasm and made him a passing hero. Opportunities abounded for thrill seekers. Various small excursions along the Southern coasts involved volunteers in high danger; witness the small but spectacular expedition of Lt. William B. Cushing, October 17–18, 1864, in which he rammed and sank the feared Rebel ironclad *Albemarle*.

Standard naval doctrine expected navies to fight navies in big, sprawling battles between heavy-gunned ships of the line—a theory that narrowed some naval views in the early years of the war. Most Federal operations were on blockading station or in combined river operations. But there were some "real" battles.

Secretary Welles contracted for some of the new ironclads shortly after he took office, and that visionary gamble brought important results at Hampton Roads. There the first battle between ironclads occurred. When the Confederates captured Norfolk Navy Yard, they raised the *Merrimac,* encased it in armor, renamed it the CSS *Virginia,* and sent it to clear off coastal blockaders. On March 8, 1862, this giant, commanded by Capt. Franklin Buchanan, steamed to attack the Union blockading squadron at Hampton Roads. Moving right into the large wooden ships, *Virginia* rammed and shelled the USS *Cumberland*, sank it, and then destroyed the USS *Congress*. Apparently impervious to enemy fire, the *Virginia* became, for that day, queen of the Civil War at sea. One of Welles's ironclads appeared in Hampton Roads that night, a small, low-lying craft with flat deck almost awash and crowned with a round turret–it looked like a "cheese box on a raft" to some, to others like a "tin can on a shingle." Almost unseaworthy, the *Monitor* nearly foundered on the way to Hampton Roads. But on March 9 she engaged *Virginia* for several hours in a close-fought duel that resulted in both vessels withdrawing without real injury. The day of the iron warship had arrived–all wooden navies were suddenly obsolete.

Another classic encounter involved Adm. David G. Farragut in a famous attack on Mobile August 5, 1864. During that battle against both Rebel ironclads and mines ("torpedoes"), Farragut had himself lashed to his flagship's rigging and gave a famous attack order: "Damn the torpedoes, full speed ahead!"

Diplomatic issues compounded some Federal naval activities. Lincoln and Secretary of State Seward were determined to isolate the Confederacy, to deprive it of any foreign aid. This involved some high-tension clandestine activity in foreign capitals, where Southern agents sought to buy blockade-runners and warships. Occasionally Union warships would lay off neutral ports to intercept Confederates vessels, or presumed Confederate vessels, often to the irritation of host countries. The practice, though, did often inhibit Southern activities and showed considerable international deference to the United States Navy.

Lincoln, Secretary of War Stanton, and Welles, together, worked to coordinate land, sea, and river activities. By 1864 combined operations had achieved remarkable sophistication and constituted a new dimension of war.

Welles deserves much credit for his evenhanded, progressive administration of the navy department. Organization and management were his strengths, and he created and ably led a huge bureaucratic structure with minimum confusion. Perhaps his amateur sailor's status helped; for him, there were no sacrosanct precedents, and innovations held no terrors.

Audacity counted far more poignantly in Confederate navy leaders. As with the army, inferior numbers demanded vision and innovation. Jefferson Davis's choice as navy secretary irritated some mem-

Officers on deck of the U.S.S. *Monitor*

bers of the Provisional Congress. Stephen R. Mallory's birthplace, Trinidad, may have triggered latent congressional Know-Nothingism. But he grew up in Key West and had been one of Florida's senators when the state seceded. As chairman of the Senate Committee on Naval Affairs, he had worked to modernize a service rusted in the past. Unfortunately, he had a look of slowness to him that bred more anxiety than faith.

Many students of the Confederacy consign him to the usual middling rummage of Davis's cabinet. Viewed from the standpoint of the resources he commanded and the loom of his opponents, Mallory's achievements rank him among the best navy secretaries in American history. Without shipbuilding facilities of consequence, once Norfolk and New Orleans fell, and without machine shops capable of making sound marine engines, with ample but scattered naval stores in the South, with most men wanting to join the army, Mallory's challenges dwarfed those facing Gideon Welles. Aware of the South's relative disadvantage by conventional measures, Mallory became one of the real naval innovators. He had a kind of restless intuition that sometimes led to outlandish things but mostly steered him to sound ideas and brilliant novelties.

Early in his tenure he said that "I regard the possession of an iron-armored ship as a matter of the first necessity," and when the *Merrimac* came into Confederate hands, he pressed its speedy conversion. Other ironclads received his money and attention, including the iconoclastic railroad ironclad *Arkansas,* until the small Southern navy had a respectable number of the latest things in naval combat—albeit most of them lacking efficient engines.

Naval ordnance also earned Mallory's early eye, and he stimulated development of the torpedo bureau, which produced numbers of mines that did deadly duty against many Federal hulls. More ships were lost to these "infernal machines" than to regular combat.

Various efforts to provide vessels to defend the navigable rivers were generally unsuccessful. Mallory tried to use Confederate marines and "cotton clads" for river defense, but these ventures were mostly overwhelmed by superior numbers.

Mallory tried to have the navy cooperate in resisting combined Federal river operations. Some Confederate naval gunners served important land batteries—notably at Drewry's Bluff—and Confederate marines helped protect ships under construction.

Confronted with the fact that the South could not compete with the Union war fleet, Mallory supported President Davis's reliance on the old American practice of privateering. Since the United States had not agreed to banning privateers under the Declaration of Paris, the Confederacy legitimately inherited the right to use these "militia of the sea." Northern outrage against this "inhumane" practice merely cloaked irritation at its being used against the Union. Many would-be privateers signed up as soon as allowed in May, 1861, and initial seizures were impressive; but the practice faded as coasts were interdicted and prizes could not be brought into the Confederacy.

Confederate cruisers posed one of the most difficult challenges to Gideon Welles's navy. Buying some ships, ordering others abroad, the Confederate navy concentrated on commerce raiding. Some of the ships in this service were fine fighting vessels, often commanded by daring and resourceful captains. These cruisers usually avoided battle against heavier warships—but not always. Various efforts were made to track them and trap them in neutral harbors—in one case, a raider was taken out of a Brazilian harbor, with diplomatic repercussions—and to fight them where found.

If the Confederacy could hit commercial shipping hard enough, Federal ships might be diverted from the blockade to relieve the merchantmen. With that in view, and also with a view to unfurling the Confederate banner round the world, Mallory supported the construction and purchase abroad of commerce raiders. They were not unknown to war; their success depended on leadership, morale, and the stoutness of the ships. Many were commissioned, and some reached the high seas. Famed far and wide were the CSS *Sumter,* CSS *Alabama,* CSS *Florida,* CSS *Shenandoah,* and CSS *Stonewall.*

Their captains are inseparable from these fast, well-armed, rakish cruisers, which accounted for many Northern ships and millions in prizes. *Sumter* and *Alabama* were commanded by Raphael Semmes, an officer of long and prosaic duty in the "Old Navy." Much like Stonewall Jackson, Semmes rested on arms for his moment, and when it came, he seized it and became one of the great sea raiders of history. He looked like a rascal, high forehead framed by long hair, eyes sunken below fierce, dark brows, his nose accented by a stiff and twisted moustache. Semmes had a gentleman's manners and a corsair's heart. In the *Sumter* he sailed for six months in the Atlantic and Caribbean, received honors from neutral ports, and captured eighteen ships. Trapped at Gibraltar, Semmes abandoned the *Sumter.* His great days were ahead.

President Davis had dispatched Capt. James D. Bulloch to England to contract for warships, cruisers, and blockade-runners. His surprisingly successful activities in the nether world of diplomatic infighting, and those of other agents, produced contracts for big and little warships and for myriad blockade-runners from Liverpool and Glasgow. The Laird Rams were his prime hope, frustrated when the United States frightened Great Britain into impounding these two ironclad marvels. His great success was a stray ship constructed in Laird yards under her way number, *290.* Federal agents suspected her purpose, but could not prove it before she left on a shakedown cruise. A modern vessel, *290* had every essential for a cruiser—a thousand tons, more than 200 feet long, and, most importantly, two 300-horsepower engines in addition to sail. Making quickly for the Azores, she received her armament, ammunition, and a mixed crew (with many Yankees). On August 24, 1862, off the island of Terceira, her new captain took charge.

For two years Semmes and his *Alabama* scourged the high seas. He coursed the Atlantic and the Gulf of Mexico (where he sank the USS *Hatteras*), to Oriental waters and to Cape Town, and back to the Azores. He finally lost her in a fight with USS *Kearsarge* June 19, 1864, off Cherbourg, France. He might have been consoled by his record, as he and his men sought ways back to the Confederacy: one ironclad warship (100 tons heavier) sunk, sixty-two vessels captured.

Other cruisers did direct damage, too, but their real impact was on fear in the North. Insurance rates soared, and a general "flight from the flag" took more than seven hundred American ships to the protection of the British ensign. These raiders set an important precedent that the Russian czar's navy tried to emulate before the First World War.

Blockade-running posed a special problem for the Confederate navy. Nominally a private matter, blockade-running often brought a fortune for one or two successful trips to and from Bermuda and Wilmington or Nassau and Wilmington, occasionally Havana to Mobile or Galveston. This lifeline became so vital that several government agencies became involved in running their own ships through the blockade. Control of free space on these coveted runners intruded on the freedom of commerce, but a beleaguered Confederate congress approved partial nationalization of space on incoming and outgoing ships in early 1864. When the ordnance department, under the able general Josiah Gorgas, bought several runners and ran them in conjunction with the medical and quartermaster departments of the war department, Mallory worked to enhance their efforts. He encouraged by official leaves the participation of Confederate naval officers in the blockade-running effort. Several served as captains on nerve-racking voyages through the Union naval curtain.

The trips were important not only in sustaining a flow of essential supplies, but also in boosting the zest of participants. A careful organization underlay the blockade-running effort. Depots in Bermuda and Nassau received freight from England and the continent; broken in the islands, shipments were transferred to blockade-runners for the run to the Confederacy.

The high risks for higher profits were run by a kind of shadow cast of captains and crews unknown save to sponsors and to daring. A successful run in and out might pay for the ship; several runs would indemnify disaster; and anyone whose nerve ran high never got enough.

"The night proved dark," Tom Taylor of the blockade runner *Banshee* recalled in his memoirs (pp. 48–54),

> but dangerously clear and calm. No lights were allowed – not even a cigar; the engine-room hatchways were covered with tarpaulins, at the risk of suffocating the unfortunate engineers and stokers in the almost insufferable atmosphere below. But it was absolutely imperative that not a glimmer of light should appear. Even the binnacle was covered, and the steersman had to see as much of the compass as he could through a conical aperture carried almost up to his eyes. . . . We steamed on in silence except for the stroke of the engines and the beat of the paddle-floats, which in the calm of the night seemed distressingly loud; all hands were on deck, crouching behind the bulwarks; and we on the bridge, namely, the captain, the pilot, and I, were straining our eyes into the darkness. . . . And fortunate it was for us we were so near. Daylight was already breaking, and before we were opposite the fort [Fisher] we could make out six or seven gunboats, which steamed rapidly towards us and angrily opened fire. Their shots were soon dropping close around us; an unpleasant sensation when you know you have several tons of gunpowder under your feet. . . .

Such excitement roiled the blood and made addicts of even careful men.

How important was blockade-running? Ratios of successful runs are impressive: in 1861 blockaders caught one out of ten runners; in 1862, one out of eight; in 1863, one out of four; in 1864, one out of three; in 1865, after most Confederate Atlantic ports were gone, one out of two. Only estimates can be made, but they indicate it was one of the Confederacy's most successful ventures: 330,000 small arms imported for the government from 1861 to 1865; 624,000 pairs of boots; 378,000 blankets. During the one-year period from December, 1863, to December, 1864: 1,933,000 pounds of saltpeter; 1,507,000 pounds of lead; 8,632,000 pounds of meat; 520,000 pounds of coffee, plus much more uncategorized material (Vandiver, *Confederate Blockade Running Through Bermuda*, pp. xxxi–xxxii, xxxvii–xi). Quite simply, blockade-running extended the Confederacy's life for at least two years.

Some commercial freighters reached Matamoras, Mexico, which remained open throughout the war. These almost direct shipments to Texas helped sustain the Confederate Trans-Mississippi Department.

Did Mallory's efforts fail? In the sense that they did not prevail over Federal fleets, or succeed in defending the rivers, yes. An overall view, though, shows that Mallory's innovative efforts – to include the rudimentary submarine *H. L. Hunley,* which sank an enemy ship – changed the nature of naval war and opened the vision of navies around the world. If he did not secure Confederate independence, he did free the naval mind of shackling inhibitions.

Full appreciation of the impact of navies did not come until war's end. During the hectic first year, both Welles and Mallory struggled for more ships and sailors as both sides settled into the war.

CHAPTER SIX

The Western Alternative

Both Lincoln and Davis looked on the middle border as a strategic area. Lincoln felt that losing Tennessee, Kentucky, and Missouri might be tantamount to losing the war. Davis knew that the Confederacy needed some of those states – preferably all – to solidify the northern border and Confederate national spirit. Lincoln counted on a groundswell of Unionism to hold the border; Davis, on sweeping Southern nationalism. Both were right and wrong.

There were divided loyalties in each of the border states. People in east Tennessee thought much like western Virginians, but pro-Secessionists prevailed – despite some loud radicals like "Parson" William G. Brownlow in favor of the Union. The state was admitted to the Confederacy in May, 1861. In Kentucky sentiments were spread fairly evenly across the state. Secessionist governor Beriah Magoffin, who stoutly rejected Lincoln's call for troops, sought for the state a neutral's profiteering status. This persisted until Confederates, under Gen. Gideon Pillow, on orders from Gen. Leonidas Polk, entered the state in September and triggered an active struggle for military control. When the Federals finally prevailed, a rump Kentucky government joined the Confederacy in December.

Missouri had a pro-Secessionist governor and majority in the legislature; Saint Louis, though, had a pro-Unionist majority and was the state's power center. Federal troops, influenced by zealous Brig. Gen. Nathaniel Lyon, held that city firmly for the Union. Lyon steadily pushed Missouri troops and some Confederate allies under Gen. Sterling Price toward Springfield, Missouri. A pitched battle raged near there on August 10, 1861–variously known as the Battle of Wilson's Creek, Oak Hill, or Springfield–in which Lyon was killed. Defeated, Union forces retreated to Rolla and yielded a large part of the state to the Confederates. Gov. Claiborne F. Jackson moved the state government from Jefferson City toward Springfield and set up a Confederate state capital at Neosho. Missouri officially joined the Confederacy late in November, 1861. Large Union forces gathered against Price and finally pushed him into Arkansas.

Probably Confederate authorities underestimated the strategic importance of Missouri. When it fell to Union control, a vital threat to the Federal right flank in Kentucky faded and a route opened to the heart of the South.

A divided Arkansas became a Confederate state with modest difficulty in May, 1861, which made it easier for the Confederacy to establish friendly relations with the Five Civilized Tribes and some of the Plains Indians in Indian Territory. Several treaties of Confederate alliance not only helped solidify the turbulent western frontier but also brought many good troops into Rebel ranks: Cherokees under Stand Watie, who received a Confederate brigadier general's commission, and Seminoles under principal chief John Jumper. These treaties were the handiwork of a colorful and under-appreciated Confederate brigadier, Albert Pike–a Mason, poet, and Indian commissioner.

President Lincoln counted heavily on pro-Union sentiment in Texas to keep the former republic loyal. Old hero Sam Houston, governor of Texas in 1861, encouraged that hope, and Lincoln thought he might connive with the former president of Texas to send arms and troops to protect the state. Houston could not deliver. A staunch Unionist himself, he resisted convening the legislature to debate secession and was at length removed from office, to be replaced by pro-Confederate Lt. Gov. Edward Clark, who presided over secession.

Houston stumped the state, predicting dire things for a Texas allied with the Confederacy: defeat, destitution, humiliation. Actually, divided purposes may have clouded Houston's activities in the secession crisis. Rumors of reviving the old society of the Knights of the Golden Circle eddied across Texas. Filibusters had long talked of a wishful kingdom with its center, perhaps, in Cuba and a golden circle with a vast circumference to include much of the deep South and Texas. A thin hint suggests that Houston may have had some lurking desire to head that amorphous empire. But he went into retirement at Huntsville, Texas, and worked to get his son a commission in the South's army. In time he came to think Confederate soldiers were among the best ever to take the field.

Military operations in the far west began with secession and spread from the Mississippi to newly created Arizona. With some exceptions, far western operations were peripheral and of slight effect. One of the exceptions, one of the two most important far western campaigns in the first year, started in Texas.

Gen. Henry H. Sibley led an expedition of some 2,500 men into New Mexico during February, March, and April, 1862, in an attempt to secure that area, open routes to the far west, and sustain Arizona Territory, which had seceded from New Mexico. A Confederate dream of holding all the southwest to California shaped Sibley's plans. A cruel march across alkali flats brought Sibley's forces into New Mexico and quick battle. At Valverde (February 21, 1862), his men skirmished with troops under Col. E. R. S. Canby and marched on to Santa Fe.

Sibley sent a probing column eastward on the Santa Fe Trail, where it fought a meeting engagement at Glorieta Pass (Pigeon's Ranch) on March 28–29, 1862, with Federal troops under Col. John P. Slough. The Yankees retreated until part of their force got behind the Rebel lines and burned their supply and ammunition wagons. Forced to withdraw, Sibley began a bitter winter retreat to Texas, and the Confederate vision of a western empire faded. Scattered fights in Arizona aimed at political results but were abortive.

Some Confederate activities in California gave brief concern to Northern authorities. Fears of a conspiracy to put California into the Confederacy were ended by prompt movement of U.S. troops. Rebel hopes for help in Nevada, Colorado, and the Montana section of Idaho Territory faded swiftly.

The other really important campaign centered on northwestern Arkansas and followed the Union defeat at Wilson's Creek. The resultant Federal build-up that pushed Price from Missouri and threatened Arkansas induced President Davis to send a dashing, competent cavalry general, Earl Van Dorn, to the Trans-Mississippi. With an army of some 14,000, including Price's men and a brigade of Indians, Van Dorn, who hoped to capture Saint Louis, fought a confused, three-day battle against Gen. S. R. Curtis's army of some 12,000 at Pea Ridge (Elkhorn Tavern), Arkansas, March 6–8, 1862. Defeated, Van Dorn gave up hope of invading Missouri and was unable to help Albert Sidney Johnston's Shiloh campaign. The transfer of Van Dorn and Price east of the Mississippi did secure the Federal flanks along the river.

Both sides throughout the war sought ways to use the west: the North to wedge it away from the Confederacy; the South to use its men and supplies and, perhaps, to use it as an avenue to the vital midwest.

A Federal invasion along the Rio Grande failed in 1862, but did succeed in occupying Brownsville. This had direct impact on the growing Confederate cotton trade (cotton traded for goods) with Matamoros, Mexico, an important harbor which remained open and under the protection of French fleet cooperating with Maximilian's imperial venture. Union troops at the mouth of the Rio Grande forced cotton trains to cross upriver at such places as Eagle Pass and Del Rio, greatly lengthening the turn-around time of wagons bringing back munitions, clothing, food, and other supplies. Galveston's occupation, together with Brownsville's, hurt Texas blockade-running in the Gulf of Mexico.

In light of Galveston's strategic and psychological importance, a Confederate campaign, under Gen. John B. Magruder, was launched and retook the city at the beginning of 1863. Brownsville was reoccupied in July, 1864.

Distance from the main war zones gave Texas, western Louisiana, Arkansas, and Indian Territory a peculiar sense of security. Federal operations were restricted to the coastline, since invasion of Arkansas and Texas posed mountainous logistical and organizational problems. Confederate activities were confined mainly to Texas Indian defense problems. As war intensified and communication became difficult with the country beyond the river, President Davis decided on a revolutionary administrative rearrangement. He sent representatives of the war, treasury, and post office departments to the newly created Trans-Mississippi Department and sought coordination of civil and military matters by assigning Gen. Edmund Kirby Smith as supercommander of everything west of the river. Shreveport, Louisiana, became the "capital" of the Trans-Mississippi.

Time, remoteness, and neglect brought a kind of whimsy to this vast area, a whimsy that took lethargic form. When Generals John Pemberton and Joseph E. Johnston sought troops from across the river to fend Grant from Vicksburg, none somehow could be gotten together, despite the fact that at least 50,000 armed and fairly well organized men were on Kirby Smith's rolls. This kind of palsy became endemic. Why? Far removed from hard war, awash in profits from trading cotton with Confederates and Yankees alike, the Trans-Mississippi could hardly afford to help the beleaguered eastern Confederacy. Not all westerners felt so selfish, but the feeling spread into a kind of western nationalism that Kirby Smith encouraged. He fought for that nationalism in the victorious battle of Mansfield, Louisiana, in April, 1864, but did not really support Sterling Price's Missouri campaign the same year. He and his area were finally converted to a different patriotism in which victory was survival. A social dry rot ran through the west, sapped energy, sloughed morals, and eroded faith in the future.

This sloughing process took time – in the young years of the Confederacy, the west apparently offered alternatives to the harshest ways of war.

CHAPTER SEVEN

On to Richmond –
And Back Again

Scarcely one hundred miles separated the opposing national capitals. That corridor between Washington and Richmond was to become America's most contested stretch of earth. Ground between the cities had military advantages for both sides. Virginia country rolled there, was cut by myriad streams, rivers; much lay hidden by forests and scrub timberland. The stately Blue Ridge Mountains ran south from the Potomac almost through Virginia and formed the eastern boundary of the food-rich Shenandoah Valley, which stretched in varying widths westward to the Alleghenies marking the lines between the eastern and western Old Dominion. All of this was just the right country for hiding big infantry formations and also for classical use of cavalry in screening and reconnaissance operations, just the right country to pique the daring of latent strategists. Each side sought the way to put northern Virginia to best martial advantage, especiallywhen armies grew wary of frontal assaults and tried increasingly the ancient art of field entrenchment.

After Manassas, Johnston and Beauregard held the Bull Run line, collected additional men, and sought to strengthen their positions with field works. Above them, again around Washington, the Federals rebuilt their army and found the second in a long roll of generals to lead it back toward Richmond.

George McClellan's ego matched the size of his new command—the Military Division of the Potomac, which came under his charge on July 17, 1861. Assignment as leader of the Army of the Potomac he accepted as homage for brilliance, proceeded to collect McDowell's wretched remnants and whip them into a large, flashy army and to perfect Washington's defenses in case the Rebels pressed their post–Bull Run advantage. As he gathered men and supplies and confidence, his dapper figure on an imposing charger was seen daily prancing around the capital as the anointed savior of the Union. His posturing angered some, but McClellan collected men like flies, trained them zealously, and won a fervent loyalty with paternal care and flamboyance.

All indicators ran well for Little Mac—an affectionate sobriquet conferred by his men. His operations in western Virginia showed him a good organizer, a sound planner, a competent strategist, and a tactician of promise. He made a lot of speeches, ordered parades galore, but he had delivered success in a vale of despond. Pomposity might be forgiven a fighter. While McClellan's manner might go against the plain grain of the president, Lincoln liked his record and hoped for the best. McClellan had no doubt of success as he prepared to invade Virginia.

He determined to use the Union's growing strength to such advantage as possible. With that in mind, he proposed to bypass Confederate lines by transporting his army by water to Urbana on the Rappahannock, where he planned to disembark and march rapidly on Richmond before Johnston could cover the capital. Lincoln had qualms but welcomed an aggressive idea.

When venerable Winfield Scott took reluctant retirement in November, McClellan took his place as general in chief of the army—he had no rival in grandiloquent promises. If Lincoln had misgivings, his general assuaged them with firmer warlike words. Still, Lincoln chafed at delays in fear of flagging Northern zeal and of too much time presented to the enemy.

Carefully McClellan built his legions, consuming time and mountains of supplies. Success, he believed, would reward care, and when he moved he wanted overwhelming superiority in his favor. McClellan's slowness through the winter sorely tried Lincoln's patience. Aware that campaigning usually stopped for the winter, the president cer-

ANOTHER GENERAL-IN-CHIEF
McCLELLAN, WITH HIS WIFE

Gen. George Brinton McClellan and his wife

tainly expected the campaign of 1862 to begin as soon as roads dried and temperatures moderated. Still McClellan honed his army, and at last it looked almost too fine to fight. He fended demands to attack until spring had almost gone. While McClellan prepared, the Confederate government worked earnestly through the winter of 1861 to fill ranks thinning from expiring enlistments, to procure and distribute arms, munitions, and other supplies—and especially to forward men to Joseph E. Johnston's army north of Richmond.

There were interesting blends of similarities between Johnston, Beauregard, and McClellan; in fact, a combination of Johnston's and Beauregard's personalities nicely duplicated Little Mac's methodical conceit. As grayclads clustered along Bull Run through the fall and winter, both Johnston and Beauregard fussed in isolation and in some rivalry over who commanded the army. Silly command arguments Davis detested and solved by sending the Great Creole to the west. Johnston's contentiousness Davis matched until relations chilled with the season. But Johnston did organize well and kept his army supplied. His worries about Federal intentions were shared by the Confederate president. Whenever McClellan moved, it seemed likely to be too soon. Men and munitions came slowly to northern Virginia, and Richmond seemed increasingly exposed.

Southern planners were not unaware of invasion avenues open to McClellan. A flanking move southeast of the capital had logic, and the Bull Run positions were too far north to permit swift adjustment. Johnston wanted to retire closer to the capital. On March 9 he fell back behind the Rappahannock River and neatly negated McClellan's Urbana Plan. Little Mac would need time to plan again.

Another Rebel general also intruded on the Young Napoleon's hopes—that solemn Presbyterian deacon "Stonewall" Jackson, whose winter operations confused a good many people. Against all precedent, Jackson decided on a winter campaign west of the Shenandoah Valley.

Sent to the valley after the Battle of Manassas, he had collected some militia forces, received a few reinforcements, and harassed Federals in the lower (northern) end of what was known as the "granary of Virginia." But as 1861's winter set in, he knew that Union forces dominated most of the state from the Ohio River to the Shenandoah Valley. How best to thwart them? A glance at a map showed that a Confederate force posted at Romney, across the Alleghenies in the South Branch Valley, would disrupt Federal railroad and highway communications and dominate northwestern Virginia. Audacity often changes odds.

Winter marching in the mountains would be severe, but the chance, perhaps, to lure McClellan into attacking Johnston before the Union army had finished preparation, the chance to clear western Virginia of the enemy, were opportunities too good to ignore — or so thought a general who measured risks against rewards. General Johnston, the department commander, and Secretary of War Judah P. Benjamin approved Jackson's scheme and sent him a few more troops. On January 1, 1862, at the head of some 8,500 men, the rumpled-looking soldier who sucked a mysterious lemon marched on Romney. Some of his untrained militia suffered, so too some men recently attached, but the campaign fuddled the Federals and satisfied Jackson.

Some of his subordinates complained directly to the war department about hardship and Jackson's "lunatic" strategy. Benjamin and President Davis blundered badly by listening out of channels, and especially in giving Jackson a direct order to bring his men back from Romney. Complying instantly with the order, he also offered his resignation in face of such lack of confidence. Johnston, also bypassed, urged charity in the midst of crisis; the governor of Virginia and many clerical friends urged restraint while they tried to explain to the government the chaos inherent in so "ruinous" a policy. In time, Jackson withdrew his resignation, his important point about command channels amply made.

He could take consolation in knowing that activity in the valley did indeed disturb Union forces. The enemy sent nearly 25,000 men against his 4,500. The ratio pleased him: he was attracting attention. Johnston wanted Jackson's little band to guard his flank, to stay between him and the Federals, delay them in the valley, and keep reinforcements away from McClellan. Jackson could attract more Yankees if he had more men, but he would do what he could. And with news that Federals were suddenly leaving the valley, Jackson took the offensive. At Kernstown, on Sunday, March 23, 1862, inadequate intelligence led him to attack a superior force, and he lost. Had fighting on the Sabbath caused the mistake? No matter, Jackson never again neglected field intelligence.

Although a defeat, Kernstown had some strategic advantage: it not only stopped Federal leakage toward McClellan, but also brought more men against Jackson. As Johnston withdrew closer to Richmond, Jackson received some reinforcements and made plans to engage the enemy. He was about to begin his Valley Campaign, a dazzling series of actions in which Jackson fought several Federal forces and beat them in detail, a campaign to give him lasting rank among the world's Great Captains.

While Jackson prepared, so did McClellan. Lincoln kept harassing his dapper general. At one point, with unvarnished irony, the president allegedly mused that if the general was not using the army, he would like to borrow it! And although keeping outward confidence in his boisterous general's new plan to embark his army for the Virginia peninsula between the York and James rivers, Lincoln took the unusual step of constructing the "President's General War Order No. 1," on January 27, which declared "that the 22d of February 1862, be the day for a general movement of the Land and Naval forces of the United States against the insurgent forces." Lest McClellan missed the point, the president issued the "President's Special War Order No. 1" on January 31, which directed McClellan's Army of the Potomac to move south of Manassas. Little Mac had to get going, Lincoln knew, or "the bottom would drop out of the whole concern."

If only McClellan would do even a little of what he promised. His plans were not all bad, but they were confounded by phantoms. Convinced he was opposed by no less than 100,000 Rebels north of Richmond, McClellan wanted at least 250,000 men in his area. Although he counted nearly 150,000 by March, he felt insecure about advancing. Lincoln, concerned that the general had too much to do, relieved him of all but his army command on the eleventh, and at last he moved.

On March 17, leading elements of his army embarked at Alexandria. Lincoln insisted on having troops left to defend Washington—a requirement soon involved in wrangling. Pressures from other sectors induced the president to siphon a few men from McClellan, but a peremptory presidential order on April 3 retaining McDowell's fine corps of 30,000 men to watch Stonewall Jackson, enraged Little Mac. He knew Washington's safety hinged on his own success and was tempted to tell Lincoln to come and fight the enemy himself. Still, he had more than 100,000 men, and Rebel defenses around Yorktown and Williamsburg seemed thinner than expected. As he moved glacially toward Richmond, his spirits rose with his rhetoric. He would have been less enthused had he known of Stonewall Jackson's doings.

Jackson had moved his little Army of the Valley up the Shenandoah to camps near Mount Jackson. Reorganization and refitting proceeded, and Stonewall kept an eye on Gen. Nathaniel P. Banks, who moved south from Winchester with about 15,000 men and counted on help from scattered Union units. Talks with General Lee, now commanding Confederate operations outside Richmond, brought Jackson encouragement and the temporary aid of Gen. Richard S. Ewell's 6,000-man division. Lee admired Jackson's dogged determination; despite rising odds, he wanted to pin all the Yankee forces west of the Blue Ridge (even west of the Alleghenies) in the mountain theater and keep them away from Richmond. They were separated and, with luck, might be defeated one by one. Finding and fixing enemy units is good tactics; beating them in detail, fine art.

In a sense, Lee measured Jackson by his achievements with a small force. Not only was General Banks returning in strength to the valley, but also Gen. John C. Frémont was inching eastward toward the Shenandoah from his Mountain Department. Lincoln, responding to Frémont's calls, detailed Gen. Louis Blenker's division from the Army of the Potomac to Frémont's army, and later, his concern rising as Jackson's movements were shrouded in mystery, he kept McDowell's corps to guard the capital. So with a few more men Jackson hoped for large results. Lee could not promise more—Johnston needed all the reinforcements available around Richmond.

Patiently Jackson fell back up the valley and made a close study of its geography and geometry. In the area north of his main base at Staunton, Virginia, the valley sat between the Blue Ridge and the Alleghenies, varied in width from ten to thirty miles, and ran northward nearly a hundred miles to the Potomac. The Shenandoah River ran northward, too, and divided at the southern base of Massanutten Mountain, a fifty-mile-long north-south range that rose some twenty-five miles north of Staunton and created two valleys—the one east of Massanutten was named Luray. Roads were not too good, although the six-foot-wide Valley Pike, connecting Staunton and Winchester, was macadamized. A skein of other dirt roads and traces created a rough parallelogram around Massanutten Mountain and in the upper and lower valley, which challenged a creative strategist.

Jackson lacked skill in understanding ground, but his brilliant topographical engineer, Jedediah Hotchkiss, gave him maps that spread the valley clearly before him. All kinds of chances beckoned. Chances shifted as Banks moved south to the end of Massanutten and threatened Staunton. In an unexpected series of moves at the end of April,

1862, Jackson apparently took part of his army toward Richmond and left Ewell in observation at a Blue Ridge mountain pass. Just southeast of the Blue Ridge, Jackson put his infantry on the "cars" and raced westward through Staunton toward McDowell, Virginia, where he joined forces with Gen. Edward "Allegheny" Johnson's 2,000-man army. On May 8 Jackson's 10,000 defeated Gen. Robert S. Milroy's 6,000 at McDowell and pursued down the South Branch Valley, sealing mountain passes eastward as they went. On May 12 Jackson moved back toward Banks's force near Harrisonburg.

Banks was in trouble. He had detached James Shield's 10,000 men toward Fredericksburg; with scarcely 9,000 left he now feared Jackson's movements. Slowly he withdrew northward toward Strasburg, which he fortified, and sent a flanking force eastward to Front Royal in hopes of preserving a reinforcement route. Meanwhile, he lost Jackson—Turner Ashby's zealous cavalry thoroughly screened the Valley Army.

Stonewall had crossed the Massanutten, moved swiftly north down the Luray Valley, and on May 23 struck and smashed Banks's outpost at Front Royal, then sent his Rebels racing to cut off Banks's retreat toward Winchester. A running engagement took the Federals into their works at Winchester, where Banks made a stand. Jackson wasted no time—his men stormed the fortifications on May 25, and Yankee remnants streamed for Harper's Ferry with Jackson in pursuit. A romantic figure of speech had it that the Shenandoah Valley pointed like a rifle barrel at the heart of the Union—but the figure now took the shape of Stonewall Jackson, and he lurked in that barrel as a seemingly unstoppable charge. As his worn and weary legions crowded toward the Potomac, the Shenandoah was clear of the enemy, and, with Shields on his way back to Banks, no help had gone to McClellan.

While Union commanders fumed at Jackson's quick marching—he had set up a system of ten minutes' rest each hour and steady pacing through a whole day—Lincoln saw a Euclidean solution to the valley problem. If Jackson's army was at Winchester, apex of a triangle, and Shields was coming into the valley at Front Royal at the right base angle, and Frémont approached at the left base angle, the two could close the base line at Strasburg and cut Jackson off as he tried to escape southward. It was, Lincoln saw, "a question of legs," and he hoped that shorter angles would put his men ahead of Jackson's "foot cavalry." Not quite. Jackson escaped, moved to the upper valley, and engaged the two forces of Frémont and Shields at Cross Keys and Port Republic during the first week of June. A double Rebel victory numbed Federal initiative in the valley, forced them back on Banks beyond Massanutten. To Lee, Stonewall reported that "God blessed our arms with victory."

The Valley Campaign remains a military classic, one studied to the present as a matchless example of what sound strategy combined with mobility, surprise, logistical planning, and determination can accomplish. In a period of forty-eight marching days, Jackson's army covered over 650 miles, fought five major battles and countless combats and skirmishes. His 16,500 men kept three enemy armies, counting more than 60,000, separated and away from Richmond, captured hundreds of Union wagons with precious supplies, and revived the Rebel victory spirit when it seemed buried in bad news. By the time the Valley Army went into the Blue Ridge for a rest, it had become legendary to South and North alike. Stonewall Jackson ranked as a new American hero. His men told affectionate jokes about him, said they expected any day to be ordered to march to the gates of Hell and take them by storm. A proud biblical parody captured a lot about the general and his men:

Man that is born of woman,
And enlisteth in Jackson's Army,
Is of few days and short rations.

"Old Jack" had kept an eye on operations around the capital; his valley fighting had been part of Richmond's protection campaign. He knew that Little Mac had landed a big army at Fort Monroe and had eased toward Yorktown; he knew, too, that Johnston had countered by moving the main Confederate army toward Richmond and sent some units to support Yorktown and Williamsburg.

By the second week of June, Jackson also knew that Johnston had been severely wounded in the Battle of Seven Pines, near Richmond, and that the fifty-five-year-old Lee now commanded the main army. That pleased Old Jack—he trusted Lee completely. And he expected Lee's summons to the capital. McClellan, moving with customary caution, inched up the peninsula. Since Johnston's attack at Seven Pines had failed, Lee reconcentrated and replanned the battle for Richmond. Lee suggested Jackson come at once. As he marched, he should keep an eye out for McDowell's corps, which might come to join McClellan from the north. Jackson should hit the Federal right, north of the Chickahominy River, cut communications, and pressure the flank while Lee's men attacked in front. Lee's call was discretionary – Jackson should decide. He went.

McClellan's amphibious movement to Fort Monroe was well planned, but he made a reckless assumption – that the Union Navy would be able to prevent interference from the CSS *Virginia* (*Merrimac*), which threatened Hampton Roads, and also help in taking Yorktown. As it happened, Federal naval forces could only neutralize the *Virginia*. That unexpected deficiency slowed the campaign, but men and supplies did get to the proposed area of operations. And McClellan had reason for some satisfaction. Army organization and management were his strengths, and the movement to Virginia showed them to best advantage.

Strategy usually came in grandiose ways to McClellan, but peninsular geography and weather conditions focused his vision. Overflowing rivers and streams reduced maneuverability in the lowlands south of the Chickahominy River, which bisected the peninsula north of Williamsburg. Despite poor maps, McClellan saw he might get between Johnston and Richmond by concentrating between the Pamunkey and Chickahominy rivers. That route would protect his base at West Point and leave an opening for McDowell, coming from the north. But he wanted to work south of the Chickahominy to attack Richmond's weaker defenses.

Confederate Gen. J. E. B. Stuart's three-day cavalry ride around the Union army, June 12–15, dismayed the Northern public as well as some of Little Mac's men – but, oddly enough, not the general. He guessed that the raid had glamour but little military value other than reconnaissance. It did alert McClellan to his exposed communications, and he prepared to change base.

The raid alerted Lee to the fact that the Yankee right could be turned, and that helped bring Jackson to Richmond. Lee, suffering a drop in reputation because of his West Virginia defeats, planned a brilliant attack, but one that probably required too much sophistication on the part of inexperienced generals and staffs. He had noted McClellan's gradual shift south of the swollen Chickahominy after the Battle of Seven Pines, noted particularly that one Federal corps, Fitz-John Porter's of 30,000 men, remained virtually isolated north of that torrent. Assuming McClellan's caution, Lee schemed to hold the main Union force in place with 25,000 men, to put the bulk of his army – 65,000 – north of the Chickahominy, and to crush Porter

Bridge repair often played a crucial role in the ability of armies to move. Here Federal troops work on a bridge across the Chickahominy River in 1862.

and roll up the Union flank in what would have been sound examples of mass and economy of force.

Jackson was to hit Porter's right flank early on the morning of June 26. As soon as he heard Jackson's guns, Gen. A. P. Hill was to advance against Mechanicsville and Porter's Union line at Beaver Dam Creek. Gens. D. H. Hill and James Longstreet were to bring their divisions through Mechanicsville, the former going to aid Jackson, the latter to support A. P. Hill. Gens. John Magruder and Benjamin Huger, holding in front of Richmond, were to demonstrate heavily and convince McClellan he dare not attack. Only the demonstrations went according to plan.

Jackson arrived late and got lost; an impatient A. P. Hill attacked Porter's entrenchments almost alone and was repulsed. While Lee pondered his next day's battle, McClellan overcame the aggressive urging of some of his generals and decided that he not only could not attack Richmond, he should hasten his change of base to the James River and consolidate his positions. Lee, on June 27, again ordered a flank attack on Porter and again saw his plans delayed.

A. P. Hill advanced at 2:00 P.M., but not until 4:00 P.M. did Jackson attack with his three divisions. Porter's corps fought fiercely and skillfully, but his line finally broke as darkness fell. His fine artillery and two brigades from Gen. E. V. Sumner's II Corps covered Porter's crossing of the Chickahominy at 4:00 in the morning of June 28.

McClellan's situation had advantages. He knew that only one of his five corps had been engaged and that it had fought well. He knew, too, that a new army, consisting of McDowell's, Banks's, and Frémont's commands, had been organized under Maj. Gen. John Pope and was ordered to his support. If the intact Federal army held where it was on June 28, Lee would soon find himself facing strong enemy forces in his front and rear. So McClellan decided to retreat to his new base at Harrison's Landing on the James.

If that decision seemed inexplicable, it hardly surprised Lee, who counted on his opponent's caution. For the moment, though, McClellan's movements baffled the Confederate leader. Where was he going? That question paralyzed Southern movements during June 28. If the bulk of the Union army moved south toward the James, Lee could cross the Chickahominy and attack. If, on the other hand, McClellan moved his men toward Fort Monroe and crossed the river downstream, Lee would have problems of recrossing. Stuart's cavalry was off raiding instead of scouting, and not until late in the day did Lee decide where Little Mac was. Longstreet and A. P. Hill were sent to hit the Federals in flank, and Jackson was ordered to press the enemy rear. Magruder's and Huger's men were to push southeastward.

McClellan himself seems to have lost interest in the battle for a time – at least his subordinates were untrammeled by his leadership during three large actions. The bulk of his force – the II, III, and VI corps – struggled on June 29 to find crossings through White Oak Swamp. Magruder, hoping for help from Jackson, hit the three enemy corps at Savage Station in the afternoon; his repulse allowed the Federals to get through the swampy barrier. Again the question ran Confederate ranks: What happened to Jackson? He apparently spent the day resting his men and rebuilding Grapevine Bridge while he could hear Magruder's battle in the distance. Why his untypical procrastination?

The obvious explanation was slow bridge repair, but that would not excuse Jackson's ignoring the sound of Magruder's fight. The real reason for the delay was an order from headquarters, signed by Lee's adjutant general, ordering Stuart's cavalry to guard bridges against enemy attempts to recross and ordering Jackson to stay at the Grapevine crossing for the same reason—and to stay put until released. Jackson obeyed, telling one of Magruder's subordinates who asked for help that he had "other important duty to perform." While Jackson waited, Federals retreated and fought with Magruder.

Next day, June 30, after crossing the swamp, the Yankees kept moving toward the James. Lee hoped to get Jackson and Huger into action to press the enemy rear from the north and to have Magruder and Longstreet pick up the attack west of the Federals as they bunched toward their base. Again Jackson delayed, this time in front of White Oak Swamp, despite the sound of battle in the near distance. Longstreet and A. P. Hill were in desperate combat at Frayser's Farm, but Jackson made no strong move to "press on" through the swamp. Instead, he dozed most of the day, apparently victim of pent-up fatigue and short rations.

A kind of weirdness tinged June 30, a Monday of errors and missed chances for the Confederates and hard fighting for the Federals, who struggled to move their wagon trains and most of their army to Malvern Hill. This strong defensive position had height for Union cannon and the advantage of proximity to Harrison's Landing. McClellan's men settled atop the hill under protection of artillery and bloodily repulsed another Rebel attack on Tuesday, July 1—an attack poorly organized and haphazardly delivered. McClellan retired that night to his base; his campaign against Richmond was over.

Casualties were appalling to a people unprepared for a war of modern artillery and improved rifles. In all of the Seven Days' Battles, Lee had over 20,000 casualties (some 4,000 killed) out of a total of nearly 88,000 men engaged. Union losses amounted to 16,000 (some 2,000 killed) out of a total of 83,000 engaged from an army of more than 115,000 men (E. B. Long, *The Civil War Day by Day,* p. 235).

Some reputations were casualties, as well—especially Little Mac's. A storm of recrimination burst over him, but he continued preaching to President Lincoln on military as well as political matters. Lincoln visited the Army of the Potomac and tried to encourage the men. McClellan was through, despite his boast that he was still near Richmond and might resume the offensive—in time.

Jackson, too, suffered. So lately a national hero, he seemed almost a failure in some eyes. During the battles Lee had scolded Old Jack in his gentlemanly way, but appeared to have no lingering ill feelings.

A Federal regiment at Gaines' Mill in the Seven Days' Battle. A black soldier sits on the ground with this Irish regiment.

President Davis seemed to have some doubts about the strange, dowdy-looking soldier, and so did some Richmond newspapers.

Capital newspapers were fickle. A few days before they had cried for deliverance, and now that the enemy no longer thronged the gates, they carped; after all, gratitude is a short-lived grace. Far from savior, Lee was pictured as nearly a villain, blamed for badly planned battles, wasted opportunities, and heavy losses.

But Lee and his generals had no time for rebuttals. While McClellan floundered around the peninsula, Gen. John Pope had collected troops and issued grandiloquent orders and proclamations, which irritated his army and angered Virginia civilians about to be subjected to illegal martial law. Originally created to help McClellan, Pope's Army of Virginia now had a new mission. When Pope moved east of the Blue Ridge in mid-July, he threatened the Gordonsville rail hub. Adhering to the basic strategy of the offensive-defensive, Lee sent Jackson to do something about Pope.

Lincoln had appointed Maj. Gen. Henry W. Halleck to the revived post of general in chief of the Union armies on July 11. Halleck had field experience in the west and had the confidence of military men. "Old Brains" (Halleck's sobriquet) decided to bring McClellan's forlorn legions from the peninsula to strengthen Pope's army – a decision McClellan detested and Pope did not clearly understand. By the time McClellan's army began a move to Aquia Creek, Stonewall Jackson had a new lease on glory.

On July 13, Jackson led his divisions toward Gordonsville. Old Jack might be the sort of man to do better in independent command. And he might be the man to beat Pope, while Lee took care of what remained of McClellan's army – the kind of strategic opportunity Lee cherished. Reinforcements went to Jackson until he counted almost 25,000 bayonets. He made good time on his march and beat Pope to Gordonsville.

Rashly Pope decided not to wait for McClellan's reinforcements and moved south. Unexpectedly, his advance under General Banks ran into Jackson's vanguard at Cedar Mountain on August 9, and a major battle developed. Badly managed on both sides, the battle ended in Banks's withdrawal. But Jackson did not pursue against all of Pope's army.

McClellan's men were arriving at Aquia by early August and were routed to Pope. Lee, knowing that Pope would be reinforced, wanted to defeat him before all of McClellan's men joined. He devised a plan to fix Pope along the Rappahannock while Jackson secretly went around his right to occupy the large Union supply base at Manassas Junction – near the old battlefield. During August 27 Jackson's men occupied Bristoe Station and Manassas Junction. Gorging on the mountainous Union supply dumps, Jackson's men filled ammunition wagons, packed four days' rations, and moved that night to a strong position in an unfinished railroad cut not too far from the Henry House Hill.

Confused by conflicting reports, short of cavalry, some of his men short of ammunition, Pope lost control of the situation. By afternoon of the twenty-eighth he decided that Jackson was at Centreville and directed his various corps there. Late in the afternoon Jackson's men attacked a Union force crossing their front – Jackson wanted to bring Pope's army down on him so that Longstreet's divisions could hit the enemy on the left flank and perhaps achieve a double envelopment. Now certain of Jackson's location, Pope concentrated.

Jackson's men stood off several attacks on the twenty-ninth and narrowly held the field at nightfall. Pope misconceived the situation and thought the Confederates were withdrawing. He ordered a pursuit, which subjected Jackson's weary men to another series of attacks, and at the crucial moment Longstreet's artillery swept across the Union advancing front. Late in the afternoon his five divisions hit Pope's army on the left rear. Pope managed to extract his troops and retreated toward Centreville—toward which Jackson, too, was moving. Through a drenched August 31 both armies groped to new positions and on September 1 a pitched engagement at Chantilly produced only casualties. But Pope was beaten. Receiving permission to fall back into the Washington defenses, his sodden legions reached the capital on September 2, 1862.

From August 27 through September 2, Pope had a total of 16,000 casualties; Lee, a total of 9,500. The war grew costlier with practice. If Confederates boasted fewer losses, they also faced a shrinking manpower pool—a cause of growing alarm in Richmond.

Alarm about men and about enemy incursions around Southern borders had forced President Davis and his new secretary of war, George W. Randolph, to ask congress to draft men for the armies— hardly a welcome proposal to individualist lawmakers. But by March, 1862, attempts to encourage reenlistments had increased morale problems in the army—liberal furlough policies had riddled the ranks, and many on leave would not come back. Rebels had learned, like their stout enemies, that war was hard. Many of them resented the physical labor of digging. Latrines were undignified enough, but trenches were used by cowards! Slaves were sometimes impressed into labor service. Bell I. Wiley in *The Life of Johnny Reb: The Common Soldier of the Confederacy* (1943), evokes the lives of Rebels with sympathy and depth.

In truth, the Confederacy's armies seemed to be melting away as spring, 1862, gave way to the dog days of summer and Yankees appeared to be winning everywhere. There were some 300,000 men in the Confederacy's armies on June 30, 1862. But the absent statistics were startling. Since the first of the year, the absent rolls had grown from 68,000 to 104,000, and almost a third of the army missed muster. So alarming were these numbers that the Confederate congress did, at last, decree conscription in April, 1862.

Union ranks were thinning, too, as enthusiasm for the field faded in ratio to exposure. Both armies had learned that life in the field lacked glamor. There were proud, parading moments when young ladies gawked in admiration at uniforms and manhood. But mostly

The Charleston artillery drew on young and old alike, as this 1863 picture shows. Conscription had begun the year before.

things were dirty, wet, hot or cold, and disease stalked camps with grim impartiality. Again it is Bell Wiley who best describes the days, joys, and sufferings of men in blue in *The Life of Billy Yank: The Common Soldier of the Union* (1952).

By the end of March, 1862, there were some 637,000 men on Union rolls, but 103,000 of them were absent from duty; the trend looked bad, since only 49,000 had been absent at the end of January. Haphazard recruiting policies and sporadic use of a growing bounty to spur bravery confused the manpower scene. Resistance to recruiters erupted here and there, especially in areas where poorer Irish Catholic laborers congregated, areas usually heavily Democratic. With increasing urgency, Lincoln called for men and for help. His energetic secretary of war, Edwin M. Stanton, called on the states for troops— some states would use their own drafts—and the president preached the need for men across the Union in every way open to him. These efforts did boost enlistments in the Army of the Potomac, as the president pondered ways to defend Washington and keep a wary eye on Maryland, which might be a Confederate objective.

CHAPTER EIGHT

The Crucial Center, 1861–62

All through the winter of 1861, pressure steadily mounted against the thin Confederate defense lines in Kentucky and Tennessee. Unconsciously pushing the Anaconda Plan, Lincoln saw the war in geographical and geometrical terms, and he read maps with a strategist's eye. When he looked at a map of the middle of the country, he was instantly struck by rivers. The Mississippi bisected the Rebel states; if it could be forced, the Trans-Mississippi Confederacy would be cut off and Davis's eastern armies dealt with piecemeal. The Ohio River ran like the lifeline of Union from western Pennsylvania to its junction with the Mississippi at Cairo, Illinois.

To Southerners, the Ohio seemed a natural northern border for the Confederacy. To Lincoln, some of its tributaries were open arteries to the Rebel heartland. As increasing numbers of gunboats joined the Union naval inventory along the Mississippi, Lincoln envisioned amphibious operations on the Tennessee and Cumberland rivers, eventually along the "Father of Waters." He had a familiar problem. Aggressive commanders were hard to find.

The president had approved McClellan's suggestion—when he was general in chief—that two departments be created in the west: the first, the Department of Missouri, including western Kentucky, should be commanded by Henry W. Halleck; the second, the Department of the Ohio, encompassing the rest of Kentucky and Tennessee, should be under Gen. Don Carlos Buell.

A moment's pondering might have raised an important question in Lincoln's mind: did McClellan pick generals like himself? If so, the new co-command structure could confound rather than coordinate.

Jefferson Davis shared Lincoln's unease about activities in the west. Too many little actions persisted, conducted by too many disorganized units. Perceiving that the area west of the mountains offered great advantages as well as weaknesses to the South, Davis grasped the need for unified command in that key sector. He had, he thought, just the man for the job—Albert Sidney Johnston. A highly trusted friend of the president's, Johnston boasted illustrious careers in the armies of the United States and the Republic of Texas. He had resigned his U.S. commission on May 3, 1861, and was appointed a full general in the Confederate Army. Confident that Sidney Johnston could organize a cohesive defense of the Tennessee-Kentucky line, Davis in September gave him command of all Confederate forces from Arkansas to the Cumberland Gap, some 50,000 men.

Johnston knew that Halleck and Buell combined in their departments about 130,000 widely scattered men. Confederate advantages were few; the best were good lateral communications. But the Federals now counted on strong naval support on the rivers and could infiltrate swiftly. Johnston's position hinged on three key points: big Fort Donelson on the Cumberland River, smaller Fort Henry on the Tennessee, and Columbus, Kentucky, on the Mississippi. He had small forces at each of these places and at several others; he delayed concentration as he pondered logistics and the moves of an army under Gen. Ulysses S. Grant.

Halleck sent Grant against the two river forts, and after an opéra bouffe affair at Fort Henry (which sat so close to the river that Union gunboats floated by and fired down into the works), Grant thoroughly dominated the timid commanders of Fort Donelson and took it on February 16, 1862, along with 11,500 men and forty cannon. His center broken, his lateral communications cut, an opportunity to defeat Grant's smaller force wasted, Johnston pondered a disaster his vacillation had certainly helped create.

General Beauregard arrived to aid Johnston and soon convinced him to concentrate the scattered Confederate units to wrest the initiative from the Federals. Johnston selected Corinth as the junction point, and Beauregard departed to take command of all Rebel troops between the Tennessee and Mississippi rivers. The Great Creole had energy and used the telegraph to coerce reinforcements from across the Mississippi and to urge help from the deep South. Beauregard saw the danger posed by Johnston's two main forces being separated by Grant and Buell, who had moved to Nashville. He urged Johnston to hasten the concentration at Corinth and moved the Columbus force in that direction, leaving a garrison at Island No. 10 that paralyzed 25,000 Union troops. Johnston, oddly enough, did not move with any special sense of urgency.

Command problems hampered Federal efforts to take advantage of their inner lines. Halleck talked of attacking "strategic points" like Memphis or Corinth, bragged about Grant's operations, but squandered the splendid opportunity to destroy Johnston's forces in detail. Buell saw the chance and wanted to join Grant and attack before Johnston got his men together. Halleck sent Grant's force up the Tennessee to raid Rebel rail lines.

Lincoln solved the command tangle on March 11, 1862, by giving Halleck command of the central theater. Once in charge, Halleck acted; he ordered Buell to join Grant's force near Pittsburg Landing, Tennessee, where the combined forces could threaten Memphis. Buell moved casually and took thirteen days to cover thirty-five miles to Columbus; a wrecked bridge there again delayed him considerably. His sloth almost lost the Battle of Shiloh for the Union.

Fortunately for Sidney Johnston, he had Beauregard to goad him and Jefferson Davis to plan for him. Davis, as much a student of war as vaunted "Old Brains" Halleck, saw the chance to hit Grant's army in its relatively isolated position near Shiloh. He began a strategic concentration of reinforcements using the latest military technology in a Napoleonic application of the offensive-defensive. The president telegraphed for reinforcements from Charleston and New Orleans, released Bragg from Mobile with his 10,000 men, and pushed them all forward by an innovative use of railroads and river steamers. By early April Johnston had 40,000 men at Corinth. Grant, unaware of enemy concentration, had encamped at Pittsburg Landing without bothering about security.

Johnston, hoping for surprise, moved his men forward under heavy security. A skirmish on April 4, 1862, seemed to have compromised

Confederate general Pierre Gustave Toutant Beauregard

the attack, but the Confederates pressed on. They found Grant's position circumscribed by the Tennessee to their right, with Owl and Snake creeks to their left. They would be attacking into a sack, but both flanks were protected and the enemy had no place to run. An early morning attack on April 6, 1862, caught most Federals unprepared. Johnston wanted to turn the enemy left and cut them off from the river. Federal positions and terrain dictated a frontal assault, weighted to the right. Beauregard had overall command of the field and botched his tactical dispositions by deploying in two lines of division with a corps in reserve. As the battle progressed, bunching along the blazing battle lines confused organization. Beauregard fed in his reserves almost evenly across the front, so there were no tactical emergency forces available to exploit opportunities. Sidney Johnston had gone forward to encourage the front. Fatally wounded, he died about 2:30 P.M. Beauregard continued to manage the advance, which had been halted by several strong points of resistance. By nightfall, the Union left had been turned, but Rebel troops were too scattered and too weary to exploit their advantage, especially against freshly massed Union cannon. During the night, Buell's men began arriving on the field.

Grant counterattacked on April 7 and slowly drove the Rebels back to the original Union positions. Beauregard retreated at the end of the day. Losses were appalling in what was the hardest fighting of the war so far–nearly 14,000 Union casualties, to 11,000 Confederate.

Disaster threatened the Confederacy. Beauregard's strength was gone. Federals controlled the Mississippi almost to Memphis. Halleck, with a large army near Corinth, had decisive victory in his grasp. It eluded him.

Beauregard's optimism persisted, and he collected reinforcements (many of them had been on the way, but too late for Shiloh). Soon he commanded about 70,000 men at Corinth, but Halleck had also collected troops and was nearby with no fewer than 120,000. Beauregard wisely decided not to try holding heavily fortified Corinth–he might simply find himself bottled up. Instead, he retired to Tupelo. Halleck, happy with having taken Corinth, left the enemy army alone.

Furious over wasted opportunities in the west, Jefferson Davis sought reasons, and Beauregard resigned his command and took sick leave. Davis gave the Army of Tennessee to Braxton Bragg on June 27, as crises compounded for the South.

Even before the impact of Shiloh could be felt fully, a decisive Federal success crowned joint naval and land efforts at the southern end of the Mississippi. For months, the Confederate commander of New Orleans, Gen. Mansfield Lovell, had called for reinforcements to strengthen the defenses of the South's largest city and most important port. Instead, he had been repeatedly ordered to send away men to help Sidney Johnston. Lovell watched anxiously a buildup of Union ships, mortar boats, and transports under Flag Officer David Glasgow Farragut and Gen. Benjamin F. Butler. To defend the mouths of the Mississippi, the Confederates counted on two large brick forts athwart the river below the city and on a barrier of hulks and chain across the river. A small Rebel fleet of wooden boats supporting the new ironclad ram *Manassas* was expected to hamper Union operations. At 2:00 A.M. on April 24, 1862, Farragut's fleet ran past the forts, broke through the barrier boom, fended off Rebel fire rafts, and reached New Orleans's docks.

A daring gamble had brought the biggest Union prize of the war. The fall of New Orleans not only had military and economic impact, but also diplomatic results. If the South could not protect so vital a city, it must be weak indeed.

Lincoln took heart. With efforts apparently succeeding to clear the Mississippi from both ends, he felt that soon the Confederacy would be cut in two. That accomplished, it might be chopped up as Winfield Scott envisioned. Davis became increasingly aware of the impossibility of defending every threatened point and sought different ways to make the offensive-defensive more effective.

In moments of dark reflection, Davis might also have pondered the qualities of his western generals. The Shiloh campaign showed good logistical planning on his own part and that of railroad and quartermaster officers. And if the president had surmounted his personal likes and dislikes, he would have seen that Beauregard had sound strategic sense and certainly more energy than Sidney Johnston. Beauregard's mercurial nature sometimes undermined his tactical sense, but he had values worth using. Bragg's part in the battle had been commendable enough, and his men had fought well—and shared no shame in defeat. Davis hoped "the only General . . . who had shown himself equal to the management of volunteers and at the same time commanded their love and respect" might somehow hold the sagging central front (quoted in Vandiver, *Tattered Flags*, p. 109). The president would try to send men from the interior, but they were scarce and demands constant.

Confederate general Braxton Bragg

For the moment the best Southern defense came from Federal inaction.

Leaving two divisions to hold Grant in place, Bragg, on July 21 began to move 35,000 men by rail from Tupelo, Mississippi, via Mobile to Chattanooga. Buell had been ordered there on June 10, but his march on inner lines was slow and plagued by logistical troubles. Bragg reached Chattanooga before Buell and considered shifting the war into Kentucky. While he gathered ammunition and other supplies, Lee cleared Virginia of Federal troops.

With Lee victorious and Bragg planning boldly, President Davis enjoyed a rare opportunity to rise above daily war necessities to think strategically. Hating the defensive, compelled to it by circumstances, he seized a chance to carry the war to the enemy. Rumor—often the best basis of statecraft—helped him plan this strategy. Winds of a conspiracy against the United States in the northwest spurred the Confederate president to gamble on a joint offensive, east and west, a gamble that might win victory or waste valuable men. But the omens seemed good. Lee, who wanted to invade Maryland, would do so; Bragg would march for Kentucky, aided by Gen. Edmund Kirby Smith's force of 10,000 men at Knoxville. Davis promised to comb the Confederacy for men in the hope that a combined attack on the Union's right and left fronts would prevent constant shuttling of troops and tend to equalize numbers. Risky indeed, his plan had great potential for wresting the initiative from the Union, for clearing Tennessee and shifting pressure into vital Federal territory. And Davis added a political dimension to his planning—overtures would be made to the people of those states to induce them to join Rebel ranks, perhaps to entice other states into the Confederacy. The invading generals would issue proclamations pledging Southern devotion to self-defense, renew the call for peace, independence, and free navigation of the western rivers, and offer liberal terms of alliance.

So bold a program would commit every reserve of men and supplies into one venture. Failure in the west could lose the Mississippi Basin; failure in the east could uncover Richmond. Success, though, could change the strategic balance of the war.

Things looked good at the start for the Confederates. As Bragg moved north from Chattanooga at the end of August and Lee crossed into Maryland in early September, Union forces were abruptly thrown on the defensive and faced depressing possibilities. Should Louisville fall, all of Indiana and Ohio would be threatened, the Baltimore and Ohio rail link would break, and Bragg might reach the Great Lakes. If Lee were not stopped, Washington might be captured and the war lost.

Lee would be bold enough. What of Bragg? Union commanders who had known him knew his personal courage, his spit-and-polish discipline, and his McClellan-like capacity to weld an army out of broken remnants. And they knew he had some kind of restless force in him. But a few surely guessed he lacked the essential fighter's spark. As he advanced from Chattanooga on August 30, 1862, he had the rhetoric for the moment. "This campaign," he said, "must be won by marching, not fighting (quoted in Vandiver, *Tattered Flags,* p. 160)." If this seemed bravado's boast, Bragg at least tried to make it true. He maneuvered Buell almost back to the Ohio without fighting, but command problems and political realities negated Bragg's great venture. Kirby Smith, an independent commander, did not join Bragg. People were not flocking to Rebel banners. Buell, who had admirably cooperated by caution, finally began to concentrate. A sharp engagement at Perryville, October 8–9 bruised both armies indecisively. But Bragg lost heart, abandoned his campaign, and marched through the Cumberland Gap all the way to Murfreesboro. Gen. William S. Rosecrans relieved Buell, and Halleck, now called to Washington as general in chief, pushed him to occupy east Tennessee.

Rosecrans moved against Bragg in late December and in the big, confused Battle of Stone's River (Murfreesboro), December 30, 1862–January 2, 1863, he won a victory of sorts. Each army suffered nearly 10,000 casualties, and Bragg withdrew toward Tullahoma, Tennessee. Rosecrans had at least held middle Tennessee, but did not advance for another six months.

In all of his campaigning, Bragg underused his cavalry. His mounted arm, under such able leaders as Joseph Wheeler and Nathan Bedford Forrest–probably the great natural soldier of the nineteenth century–could have done much better duty than allowed by Bragg's limited thinking.

So the left prong of Jefferson Davis's joint offensive had been stopped and bent back. Bragg could boast of large supplies captured, of holding the initiative for months and not losing the Confederate center altogether–but the writ for 1862 in the west ran for the Union. What of the other prong of Davis's offensive?

CHAPTER NINE

A Confederate Tide
to Gettysburg

Pope's army straggled into Washington and spilled through the city, ragged, demoralized veterans clotting the streets and shocking the populace. Lincoln, too, felt the shock. Pressure of Northern public opinion burdened him now; how many more defeats would the country tolerate? McDowell had marched off to finish the Rebels at Bull Run; McClellan marched to finish them at Richmond; Banks marched to smash Stonewall Jackson in the valley; Pope took his "headquarters in the saddle" into Virginia to help McClellan finish Lee—and now remnants of all those finishing schools roamed a flotsam through the capital of the United States of America. Things might look good in the west, but the main armies had been driven from Virginia, and criticism mounted.

Public reaction eddied out in various ways. Lincoln understood the obvious: if the public ceased to support the war, it would end. Loud arguments raged about the way he was running things, about the length and costs of the conflict, and about the nature of the Union. And not all of these were political arguments—many were serious questions raised by serious citizens. Opinion makers included intellectuals, of which the North claimed more than its share, and their various reactions tracked the national uncertainties. Certain New England clergymen, writers, and speakers–songwriters and poets, too–had developed an apocalyptic vision of the war and preached it in religious phrases and saw it as a working of the ways of God. Many soldiers gladly believed the religious promise of things they did. In late days, warriors could take comfort in Lincoln's Second Inaugural, with its acceptance of the war as holy purpose.

> Let us judge not, that we be not judged. . . . The Almighty has His own purposes. "Woe unto the world because of offenses; for it must needs be that offenses come, but woe to that man by whom the offense cometh." If we shall suppose that American slavery is one of those offenses which, in the providence of God, must needs come, but which, having continued through His appointed time, He now wills to remove, and that He gives to both North and South this terrible war as the woe due to those by whom the offense came, shall we discern therein any departure from those divine attributes which the believers in a living God always ascribe to Him? . . . If God wills that [the war] continue until all the wealth piled by the bondsman's . . . toil shall be sunk, and until every drop of blood drawn with the lash shall be paid by another drawn with sword, as was said three thousand years ago, so still it must be said, "The judgments of the Lord are true and righteous altogether."

John Greenleaf Whittier had a Quaker's opposition to conflict but became so ardent for abolition that he accepted the Civil War as God-given. Henry David Thoreau compared John Brown's hanging to the crucifixion of Christ. Stephen Foster gave biblical rank to Lincoln with his highly popular recruiting song, "We are coming, Father Abraham, three hundred thousand more." But Julia Ward Howe, more than anyone, caught the missionary zeal of the North's crusade for freedom. *The Battle Hymn of the Republic* came to her, she said, spontaneously in the night; she got up and wrote:

> Mine eyes have seen the glory of the coming of the Lord:
> He is trampling out the vintage where the grapes of wrath are
>   stored;
> He hath loosed the fateful lightning of his terrible swift sword:
> His truth is marching on.
>
> I have seen Him in the watch-fires of a hundred circling camps;
> They have builded Him an altar in the evening dews and damps;
> I can read His righteous sentence by the dim and flaring lamps.
> His day is marching on. . . .

In the beauty of the lilies Christ was born across the sea,
With a glory in his bosom that transfigures you and me:
As he died to make men holy, let us die to make men free,
While God is marching on.

Such biblicality did not reach to all. Many newspapers around
the North raged impiously at increasing waste of men and money.
Some leading writers found nothing admirable in the war; some even
found it almost anti-Christian. There is much of this in Walt Whitman's *Leaves of Grass,* an almost secular collection of often patriotic
poems. His agonized exposure to so many wounded thousands surely
quenched his sense of glory. Probably the closest he came to apotheo-
sizing was in *O Captain! My Captain!* and *When Lilacs Last in the
Dooryard Bloom'd,* and the hero is Lincoln.

Apotheosis lay far in the future for the embattled Union president as beaten veterans wandered Washington. Although Pope had
done a reasonably competent job, Lincoln knew he would have to
go. Who could command the Army of the Potomac? Who could organize the wreckage into the semblance of an army and shove it into
battle against Lee's victorious legions thronging along the Potomac,
possibly about to invade the North? Who but McClellan? His organizational skills were acknowledged even by his enemies, and the men
in the ranks loved and trusted him. Lincoln now considered him a
fine army builder but not a fighter. He could refit the army, prepare
adequate defenses for the capital, but would probably be replaced
when an offensive opportunity came. McClellan, ignorant of presidential misgivings, took the assignment while Lee pondered a new
campaign.

President Davis's military-political application of his offensive-
defensive strategy clarified some of Lee's thinking. Logistical facts
lent impetus to the idea of invading Maryland. Virginia had been
scavenged mercilessly by all the armies and had left little worth taking. Food, forage, other supplies awaited in abundance across the
Potomac. A Confederate army in Maryland would give loyal Mary-
landers a chance to join the Southern colors—as Davis firmly hoped.
A possible negative: the Confederacy repeatedly said all it wanted was
to be left alone in independence, that it had no territorial interests
outside its own boundaries. Would the joint invasions make mock-
ery of that claim? Possibly, but it could be argued reasonably that
Maryland and Kentucky were really part of the Confederacy—gray legions would be operating within legitimate borders.

Lee really had no choice and wasted little time preparing for the Maryland incursion–which left several things dangling. He did not seem to have a clear objective–save the vague possibility of moving on Harrisburg, Philadelphia, or Baltimore, cutting important Union rail communications, and hitting targets of opportunity. In his hasty planning Lee made an error in judgment. When he learned that Mc-Clellan again would be the opponent, he made the complacent assumption that his old foe would move with typical sloth. This time he was wrong.

Screened by Jeb Stuart's cavalry, Lee's men crossed the Potomac on September 4, 1862, and were near Frederick by September 7. Mc-Clellan moved slowly northwestward with 85,000 men, but had over-counted Lee's 55,000 into 120,000. He feared for Washington!

Lee divided his force. Jackson went to capture Harper's Ferry–possibly to secure the Shenandoah as a supply line; Longstreet was sent to meet a threatening Federal militia force. By September 10 Lee had scattered his army in the face of the enemy. Why this dangerous gamble? Probably because Lee believed that McClellan could not bring himself to move quickly enough to make a difference. That was a likely assumption, except on September 13 McClellan received a copy of Lee's Special Order No. 191, which outlined his whole plan of dispersal. For sixteen hours Little Mac did not move–he digested the information. But then he moved with unwonted speed.

Lee, quickly warned of McClellan's intelligence coup, made hasty efforts to reconcentrate. He sent a force to block South Mountain and ordered concentration at Sharpsburg on Antietam Creek. Mc-Clellan struck Lee's men at South Mountain while Longstreet moved toward Sharpsburg. Jackson besieged Harper's Ferry and could not join immediately. When McClellan forced the mountain, Lee prepared to hold along Antietam in relatively weak positions unstrengthened by field works and with scarcely 20,000 men on the field. McClellan arrived late on September 15. Had he attacked vigorously the next day, Lee would probably have been crushed, but McClellan waited and planned himself into fragmentation. On September 17, after Lee had been reinforced by most of Jackson's men, McClellan watched as his army delivered a series of bold and tactically sound attacks from the right, to the center, and then on the left. McClellan took no personal part in coordinating his attacks, and they went in piecemeal, nearly succeeded, and at length all were repulsed because Lee was allowed to shift men from attack to attack. He was saved

Slain Confederates lying in a cornfield at Antietam September 17, 1862, one of the bloodiest days of the Civil War

almost at the moment of defeat by the arrival of A. P. Hill's division from Harper's Ferry.

Both commanders mismanaged the Battle of Antietam (Sharpsburg). Lee's determination to stand with inferior numbers on weak ground seemed uncharacteristic and was certainly dangerous. McClellan's typical hesitancy confounded his subordinates, who were frequently frustrated in attempts to take advantage of Confederate weaknesses. Every battle seems to have its swaying moments of crisis and usually one of real decision—Antietam had many moments of Confederate crises, several of real decision, and McClellan missed them all.

Against his subordinates' advice, Lee held the field during the eighteenth, apparently hoping to lure McClellan into another attack—which probably would have eliminated the Army of Northern

Virginia. Not only did Little Mac have an unused corps available, he had received reinforcements. But McClellan did not attack and Lee retired to Virginia during that night. Of some 40,000 men on the field, Lee lost about 14,000; of McClellan's 70,000, he lost about 12,500.

On the threadbare promise of Antietam, Lincoln issued his Preliminary Emancipation Proclamation and changed the nature of the war. Great Britain turned slowly to the Northern side.

Now that the right prong of Jefferson Davis's offensive had been clipped, what strategy could retain the initiative and somehow negate the rising tide of Union numbers? Davis learned from his double offensive. Unwilling to believe that Bragg had failed of resolution, Davis fixed on faulty command arrangements as the cause of western problems. They were complicating factors, certainly; with Bragg and Kirby Smith co-equal commanders, cooperation had been difficult, and coordination from Richmond impossible. Davis, led by his brilliant new war secretary, James A. Seddon, recognized that command arrangements for the Army of Northern Virginia needed no tinkering. But the west posed vast problems that caused the two war planners to consider a new concept in military delegation, one that indicated the president and the secretary were original organizational theorists. Since geographical departments had not solved issues of rank and seniority in the field, Davis began to think of what is now called a theater command in the west.

Despite the telegraph, distance still wrapped battlefields in the "fog of war," the west in particular because of widely scattered forces. Old methods worked no longer: a deputy war leader was needed out there, a general of experience equal to the broadest authority. If he rose to his chance, he would coordinate all Rebel forces and all logistical efforts in his domain and intrude on state and local politics to military purpose. The right man would seize the heartland and rule it as his satrapy. Who? Lee had exactly the right niche. Bragg, Davis hated to admit, was marred by defeat. Beauregard—too flamboyant for the president's austerity—was back in Charleston doing brilliant work in defending the city. That left only one man of proper experience, the man Seddon had in mind—Joseph E. Johnston. Davis had qualms, Johnston may have had some, but he wanted to be back in the field and accepted the assignment in late November, 1862. Did he have the vision to see war as a military equation with two complex variables—people and power?

President Lincoln reviews the camp at Antietam, October 8, 1862. Detective Allan Pinkerton stands at left, Gen. John A. McClernand at right.

Lincoln matched Davis in pondering command problems. He thought he had arrived at the right command structure with Mc-Clellan installed as general in chief; then he thought Henry Halleck would do the job. McClellan's plans were obscurantist marvels, and Halleck wrapped himself in minutiae. So, like it or not, Lincoln was still a practicing commander in chief. But he looked for some competent military man to run the war for him. It had not yet occurred to him that he was fast becoming a master strategist as he kept his eye fixed on the whole conflict and on the enemy's armies.

As the commander in chief, Lincoln fired George Brinton Mc-Clellan—for the last time. Who could pick up the pieces after Antietam and get after Lee? Who had the sense to know that the North had more of everything, the sense to mobilize it and overwhelm the Rebels? Despairingly he turned to a gentleman-soldier, a fine corps commander in the Army of the Potomac, Gen. Ambrose E. Burnside, whose tonsorial sweep gave a word to the English language—sideburns. A rightfully humble man, Burnside said he was incompetent to command a large army and, lamentably, would prove his point. Taking command on November 7, 1862, he reorganized the Army of the Potomac and moved south toward Fredericksburg.

Lee hated losing the initiative and after Sharpsburg stayed close to the Potomac, hoping to lure McClellan into an attack. Reorganizing his army into two corps (James Longstreet commanding the First Corps and Stonewall Jackson the Second), Lee left Jackson in the valley, threatening the Union right flank, and went with Longstreet to Culpeper Court House, to confront the main enemy thrust.

Dividing the army had dangers, as recent experience illustrated, but McClellan likely would not take advantage of it, nor would Burnside. Burnside ranked as a competent corps commander, but hardly fervent. Lee might impose on him as he had his predecessor. Burnside, though, had a coherent plan of operations—not brilliant, but coherent. He wanted to concentrate near Warrenton, threaten a dash to the valley to cut off Jackson, and move the main army to Fredericksburg, where he would be between Lee and Richmond. Lee would have to come to him, and Burnside could either fight or take the enemy capital. Skeptical, Lincoln approved with the caveat that speed was essential. Burnside moved quickly to Falmouth, north of Fredericksburg, by November 17 and caught Lee out of position. Gen. E. V. Sumner urged a swift river crossing, but Burnside called for pontoon bridges and Halleck failed to urge haste on supply officers. Not until November 25 did the first bridges arrive; by then Longstreet's men disputed Rappahannock crossings.

Burnside might still have gotten between Lee's corps by a quick march up the river; Jackson could not arrive for several days. Like so many Civil War generals, Burnside focused on the wrong objective—his eye fixed on Richmond, not on Lee's army. So he waited to control the river and cross closer to the enemy capital. That decision is indefensible on almost any ground— Longstreet's men were in front, and although the Federals might well have overwhelmed them, the price would have been high. Waiting for more bridges, which is what Burnside did, simply gave Jackson time to reach the field. Obviously the Union commander should have moved upriver and threatened both wings of Lee's army, or crossed the river and moved on Richmond via the Rapidan River and Gordonsville. As Burnside waited for more pontoons in front of Fredericksburg, Lee's lines grew stronger in men and entrenchments.

A kind of eerie fatalism hung over Burnside's headquarters while Lee's legions gathered and opportunities faded. The road to Richmond seemed to lead straight through the Army of Northern Virginia, which perched mainly on high ground behind frowning earthworks. Burnside believed the erroneous reports of balloon observers that Lee had posted his army south of Fredericksburg, with his left resting opposite the town. Burnside skewed the strength of his three "Grand Divisions" to his right, arraying Hooker and Sumner against formidable Marye's Heights and Gen. W. B. Franklin on the left in open ground fronting Jackson's Second Corps. He counted on superb artillery support from the high ground across the river to sustain an attack against massed men and guns.

The attack began on the cold morning of December 13, 1862. Repeated assaults on Marye's Heights and its grisly "Sunken Road" piled up Union casualties; Franklin's attack on the left made early progress but was finally driven back without result. By nightfall the attacks waned at a cost of nearly 12,000 Union casualties to about 5,000 Confederates killed, wounded, and a few missing.

In Washington an anxious president dogged the military telegraph and heard again of high hopes dashed in gore. Another defeat, another wasted campaign, thousands more dead as winter seemed to freeze the nation's hope. In Richmond a grateful president congratulated a victorious general as he rested his legions and begged for food, firewood, and simple comforts for men suffering a cold and hungry winter on the Rappahannock.

Lee hoped fighting had ended for the year, but Burnside, scorched to the high anger of a timid man, tried one more tilt for glory. Late in January, 1863, he ordered a flanking movement upriver from Lee, only to endure a charade of his men losing the campaign to Virginia mud. Derisive comments from his subordinates nearly maddened Burnside, who lashed out with threats of dismissal. Sadly Lincoln relieved the humble general on January 25 in favor of Gen. Joseph

Hooker–proudly known as "Fighting Joe." Lincoln hoped for truth in the label.

Hooker received from Lincoln an intriguing order of appointment, one filled with the president's personal brand of honest criticism and aimed at bristling pride. Lincoln told him that

> there are some things in regard to which, I am not quite satisfied with you. . . . You are ambitious, which, within reasonable limits, does good rather than harm. But I think that during General Burnside's command of the Army, you have taken counsel of your ambitions, and thwarted him as much as you could, in which you did a great wrong to the country, and to a most meritorious and honorable brother officer. I have heard . . . of your recently saying that both the Army and the Government needed a Dictator. Of course it was not *for* this, but in spite of it, that I have given you the command. Only those generals who gain successes can set up Dictators. What I now ask of you is military success, and I will risk the Dictatorship. . . . I much fear that the spirit which you have aided to infuse into the Army, of criticizing their Commander, and withholding confidence from him, will now turn upon you. I shall assist you as far as I can, to put it down. Neither you, nor Napoleon, if he were alive again, could get any good out of an Army, while such a spirit prevails in it. . . . And now, beware of rashness.–Beware of rashness, but with energy and sleepless vigilance, go forward, and give us victories.

Hooker overlooked this presidential homily in the fullness of fortune. With characteristic energy he plotted Lee's destruction–and he plotted well. He would fix Lee in the Fredericksburg lines with part of his army, take the main body to an upriver crossing, swing around the Confederate left, and get between Lee and Richmond. Aware that Longstreet, with two of his divisions, had been detached to the south as a guard against Federal incursion on Richmond from the Virginia peninsula and as a foraging force in North Carolina, Hooker determined to use his much larger numbers to force the Rebels to fight on Yankee terms. He began his campaign swiftly in late April, 1863, as spring greened the Rappahannock Valley and roads dried and spirits rose.

Anticipating action from Fighting Joe, Lee quickly grasped his strategy and on April 30 ordered Jackson to intercept the enemy in or near the Wilderness of Virginia, that great, gloomy, wooded area stretching west and south from Fredericksburg. When Jackson's men moved into the Wilderness to catch Hooker before he cleared the

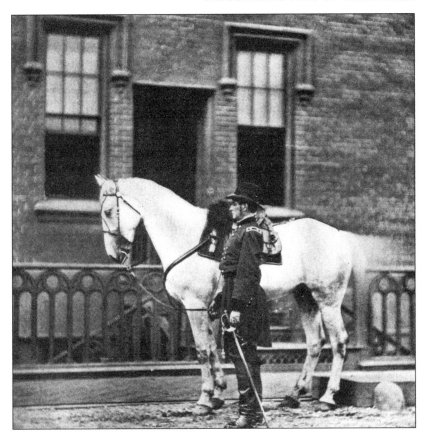

Joseph Hooker

woods, the Battle of Chancellorsville began – a battle forever famous as a classic in maneuver and applied psychology.

Hooker's dispositions were excellent; when he reached Chancellorsville, he might be able to get between Jackson's men and Gen. Jubal Early's screening force at Fredericksburg. Greatly outnumbering both enemy forces, Hooker could beat them in detail. He squandered the opportunity as the dank, dripping woodland worked its alchemy of dread. Jackson's probe on May 1 stalled the Yankees; Hooker entrenched and yielded the initiative. Lee and Jackson sought ways to negate the heavy log works the Yankees had constructed. Could a way around Hooker's right be found? Yes. A fairly well covered road led all the way around the Union army. Jackson received his most exciting orders from the general he would follow anywhere. Take

28,000 men, flank Hooker while Lee held the front with a scant 16,000 grayclads.

One of the great flank marches of military history began at 8:00 A.M. on May 2, 1863. The Second Corps of the Army of Northern Virginia marched some fifteen miles across Hooker's front and around his army and hit it from behind. Security cracked several times during the march; some Federal troops attacked the column and reported a mass of Rebel infantry to Hooker—who concluded that Lee was retreating to Richmond.

When Jackson attacked at 5:15 P.M., the Union right crumbled and spilled into Hooker's rear area. He tried to rally an artillery defense, but the Rebel attack remorselessly rolled on. At a critical point in the action, Fighting Joe was leaning against a column on the porch of his headquarters when it was struck by a Rebel shell. Knocked senseless, Hooker recovered slowly but refused to yield command. And although competent subordinate leadership saved his army and provided an opportunity to attack, Hooker lost his nerve.

Jackson's attack stalled with nightfall, and he rode ahead of his lines to find enemy positions. Riding back to his troops, he was fired on by nervous Rebel infantry, wounded, and carried from the field. Command passed finally to Jeb Stuart as the senior general present. Stuart renewed the attack with morning, as did Lee. Hooker's men were now fortifying and fighting stubbornly. Hearing that Gen. John Sedgwick's corps had driven Early out of the Fredericksburg lines and convinced that Hooker had gone on the defensive, Lee left Stuart with 25,000 to hold the Wilderness and took 21,000 to deal with Sedgwick. With speed and daring, a whole Union corps might be cut up and captured.

Battle weary, hungry, and working in hard ground, Lee's and Early's men were slow and ragged in their attack on Union positions west of Fredericksburg. Sedgwick escaped. But Lee still hoped to finish Hooker and planned a final attack on May 6—a rash idea, since the whole Federal line now was heavily entrenched. But Hooker recrossed the Rappahannock during the night of May 5–6. His great venture to Richmond cost 17,000 casualties to Lee's 13,000.

How assess Chancellorsville? It crowned the cooperation between Lee and Jackson and stands as a signal Southern victory. Hooker never used all his force. He lost his nerve; the knock on the head only addled an already broken psyche. Lincoln, too, nearly broke. When he heard the news, he cried out in anguish: "My God! My

Stonewall Jackson, April, 1863

God! What will the country say?" (quoted in T. Harry Williams, *Lincoln and His Generals,* p. 242). The North would rage. But the South would mourn the costliest victory of the war: on May 10, 1863, Stonewall Jackson died. He was thirty-nine years old. Jackson had been Lee's right arm.

Lincoln pondered a complex problem of morale versus failed men, failed opportunities, and failed ideas. The Army of the Potomac, beaten again, was made of firm stuff; its body battered, but heart sound, it would fight for a good leader. Some of the men wanted Little Mac back; he, at least, had stopped the Rebs at Antietam. Some of the men wanted to go home—the war seemed hopeless. And there were some who thought they could whip Lee, given a fighting chance. Hooker, for a time after Chancellorsville, acted like a general. A thorough refitting and reorganization put his army in top shape, and he kept close watch on Lee. Hooker, Halleck, Lincoln all thought Lee would do something aggressive. What? Where?

Those questions engaged President Davis, his cabinet, and senior military advisors while Lee recruited, refurbished, and reorganized the Army of Northern Virginia. Jackson's death left a chasm in command. Lee now divided his army into three corps: Longstreet kept his solid First; Jackson's famed Second went to his trusted lieutenant, Dick Ewell; the new Third was given to Ambrose Powell Hill. Ranks swelled with conscripts and new units from the deep South; supplies filled the depots—though rations were thin—and Stuart's horses were rejuvenated. What should this resplendent army do?

Longstreet, noting that the South still had interior lines, suggested Bragg be reinforced to crush Rosecrans. That would surely call Grant from Vicksburg. Beauregard thought relief of Gen. John C. Pemberton, besieged in Vicksburg, essential to defeat Ulysses Grant and save the Mississippi. Lee saw logic in both schemes but kept his own focus on the Virginia theater and suggested that an invasion of Pennsylvania would relieve his army as well as Vicksburg by putting pressure on the sorest point of the Union—Washington. Lee's power prevailed, and he prepared to move north. Hooker understood strategy and sifted intelligence well; by late May he suspected Lee planned to move down the Shenandoah, either to flank him back to Washington or to recross the Potomac. Gen. Alfred Pleasanton's horsemen went in search of Lee, and had a meeting engagement with Stuart's full force at Brandy Station on June 9.

Brandy Station swirled into the biggest cavalry action in American experience. Confused, seesawing, hectic, the battle engaged about 10,000 men on each side in shooting, hacking, and charging until late in the day, when Stuart's men began to prevail—especially after some foot soldiers arrived to help. Pleasanton retired, encouraged by near victory, and gave Hooker vital information: Rebels were in force near Culpeper, and it looked as though Stuart had been preparing to move.

Lee's vanguard crossed the Potomac in mid-June, headed for Chambersburg, Pennsylvania. Hooker, using his own inner lines, took his army toward Frederick, Maryland, a location covering Washington and also threatening Lee's communications. Hooker's reactions to Lee were sound, but Lincoln had lost confidence in him. Worse, Hooker was losing grip on himself. Clearly he was afraid to fight Lee. Like McClellan, he fantasized enemies in Washington, felt hugely outnumbered, and resented interference with his army. In a fit of pique, he asked to be relieved, and Lincoln hastily complied. On June 27, 1863, the command went to Gen. George Gordon Meade, Pennsylvanian, veteran corps commander, competent, plodding soldier of nervous demeanor, fiery temper, and considerable personal fortitude. Surprised at the assignment, Meade took it as a duty. Ordering the army north from Frederick, he hoped to catch Lee at a scattered disadvantage.

That summed Lee's situation fairly well. His army spread across a big part of southern Pennsylvania from Chambersburg to Carlisle to Harrisburg and York. And his Rebels were wallowing in the rich farmland's food and forage. They heard rumors of hats and shoes at Gettysburg, and those rumors stirred trouble. Rumors were curiously hard to check. Stuart, acting under Lee's usually permissive orders, had gone off on a wagon hunt in Maryland – probably trying to assuage the scars of Brandy Station – and the cavalry still with the main army had been spread too thin for sound reconnaissance.

Lee pulled his army toward Cashtown which had strong defensive positions and which sat on the flank of an advancing Union force. But some of A. P. Hill's men marched toward Gettysburg in search of shoes. At about 8:00 A.M. on July 1, Hill's men ran into strong resistance just northwest of Gettysburg. A Union cavalry division, carefully deployed with good artillery support, confronted the Confederates. Troops of both armies piled up around the town, and a major battle began without either army commander's intent.

For three days a bitter, bloody battle raged around Gettysburg. Several times Lee attacked, several times he was repulsed – once in the bare nick of time. A fearsome, grueling testing of both armies finally culminated in one of gallantry's last great gestures – Pickett's Charge. George Edward Pickett of flowing locks and poetic soul led 15,000 men against Meade's well-entrenched center on July 3. It was a splendid effort, one of flying banners, precision marching, storms of grape and canister sweeping over the attackers, of gaps and fallen

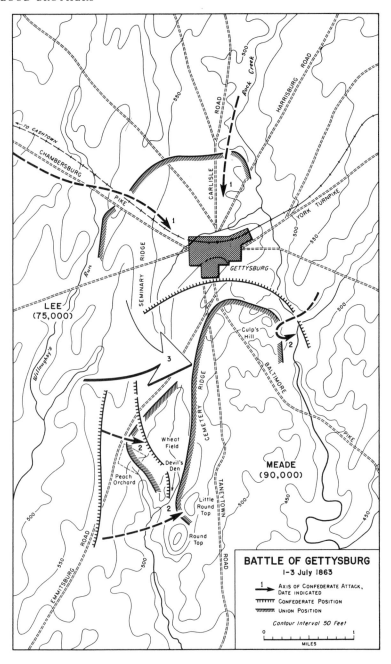

BATTLE OF GETTYSBURG
1–3 July 1863

1 ▶ AXIS OF CONFEDERATE ATTACK,
   DATE INDICATED
▁▁▁▁ CONFEDERATE POSITION
▁▁▁▁ UNION POSITION

Contour Interval 50 Feet

0 ————————— 1
        MILES

Dead Confederate youth in the "Devil's Den" at Gettysburg

and a few men who broke through the blue lines—and of the shattered survivors who streamed back, shocked, torn, and maimed. It was America's greatest battle.

It was Lee's worst. Confederate casualties neared 21,000 to the Federals' 23,000—almost a third of Lee's army had been killed, wounded, or captured. He escaped total destruction only because Meade failed to counterattack or to push the Confederate retreat—and that failure grievously wounded President Lincoln. Another Antietam, another great chance gone! Who could win a decisive battle? Jefferson Davis rejected Lee's suggestion of relief: he had no greater general. But somewhere in the dark recesses of a presidential muse a question must have festered: what had gone wrong? Presidents are often isolated but not long fooled—word came of a different Lee at Gettysburg, a petulant, stubborn man, heedless of "Pete" Longstreet's proposal to flank Meade, an ill man the day that Pickett's men marched into death and history, a superior sharply demanding obedience to orders some found futile. But when those broken 5,000 came down that searing slope, the old Lee snapped back in tender, guilty anguish. "All this is my fault," he quietly confessed to those faithful remnants who still would follow him (quoted in Vandiver, *Tattered Flags*, p. 225). Lee's return to normal loomed more vital now than ever to a country shattered by the first week of July, 1863. Not only did the South suffer Gettysburg that week, but also it suffered the loss of Vicksburg and its 30,000-man garrison. With that bastion went effective connection with the Trans-Mississippi. Out there in the west it might just be that the war was being won and lost.

CHAPTER TEN

Vitality at Vicksburg and Chattanooga

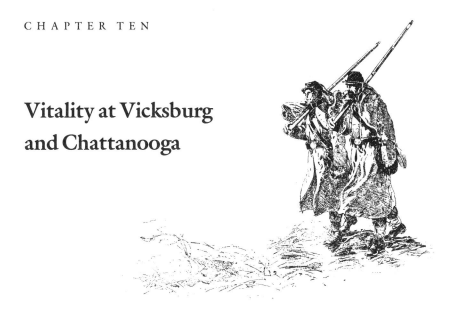

Meade's failure put Lincoln in deep gloom. To his secretary, John Hay, he poured out furious anguish in wake of Lee's escape after Gettysburg (reported in Williams, *Lincoln and His Generals,* pp. 268–69). "We had them within our grasp. We had only to stretch forth our hands & they were ours." He had expected this news, he despondently told Navy Secretary Gideon Welles. "And that, my God, is the last of this Army of the Potomac! There is bad faith somewhere. . . . What does it mean, Mr. Welles? Great God! What does it mean?" In a familiar way of teaching and venting, Lincoln wrote a long letter to Meade, possibly the toughest he ever wrote to a general. He filed it, unmailed, probably fearing it would do more harm than good to an earnest, willing soldier.

The letter, though, showed the president advanced far beyond most military minds in a firm grasp of the war. The first week of July Lincoln knew was the turning point: two Rebel armies were exposed, and armies were the main objectives. Had Lee been smashed as Vicksburg fell, the stuffing would have gone out of the Confederacy. "As it is," Lincoln mourned, "the war will be prolonged indefinitely." He did not relieve Meade—who was better? But he had little faith that the Army of the Potomac could do more in Virginia than it had in Pennsylvania; he doubted Meade could win in an offensive battle with Lee.

As Lincoln looked for consolation, he saw one bright sign. U. S. Grant had gumption. When he fixed on an enemy, he stuck. That grizzled, disheveled soldier without grace or much couth chewed on his cold cigar as he chewed on the enemy and kept going forward. Once detached from Buell, Grant fixed on Vicksburg and tried various ways to get it. That great Confederate bastion with heavy cannon dominating the Mississippi, combined with the smaller, no less vital, Port Hudson, downriver, served to hinge the Trans-Mississippi Department to the eastern Confederacy. Vicksburg deserved all the attention both sides lavished.

While Grant had his own schemes for taking one of the key sites of the South, he had considerations other than military necessity working on him. Forced to react to political and journalistic carping, he tried four different approaches to the South's vital Mississippi fortress; all four failed—one to a daring cavalry raid by Earl Van Dorn—but Grant kept at it. By late April his cooperating gunboat fleet had passed Vicksburg's batteries, and he moved a large force along the west bank of the Mississippi to find a promising crossing point where he would use his gunboats again. By the first of May, Grant had recrossed the Mississippi and turned north to get between Gen. John C. Pemberton's defenders of Vicksburg and Joseph E. Johnston's small force at Jackson, Mississippi. Grant had produced!

Productive aggressiveness set him far apart from his colleagues. Lincoln always looked for generals who did well on their own and kept grinding on the Rebels. If Grant took Vicksburg, he would achieve the greatest strategic victory since the fall of New Orleans. It took a good deal of marching and some hot fighting, but finally he did it. He had fought Pemberton in a pitched battle at Champion's Hill, won it, and invested the Confederate fortress city on May 18. He made a quick, violent assault on Pemberton's formidable works May 19 and was bloodily repulsed. Grant wanted to beat Pemberton quickly, not only so that he could hit Johnston before he was strengthened, but also so that he could swing south to aid Gen. N. P. Banks in his siege of Port Hudson, the last Confederate fort commanding the Mississippi. A renewed attack on Vicksburg's strong works failed on May 22, costing Grant 3,200 casualties.

Grant now moved to get between Johnston's force and Pemberton's. Johnston, trying to save the garrison, pondered how to relieve Vicksburg. Pushed out of Jackson, he gathered a thin force north of Mississippi's capital at the apex of a right-angle triangle, with Vicksburg and Jackson the left and right anchors of the baseline. About thirty-five miles from Pemberton's works, Johnston strove to build up his army and, on May 17, ordered Pemberton to evacuate Vicksburg and save his army. A council of war and President Davis advised Pemberton to stay put—Vicksburg had strategic and morale importance far beyond its military potential. Johnston continued working to scavenge men from a war department trying to help both Lee and Bragg.

Grant's siege ground on until July 4, when Pemberton surrendered —hoping for generous terms on Independence Day. He got none, save the paroling of himself and his army. On July 9, the small, heroic garrison of Port Hudson surrendered to Banks. Johnston, moving toward Vicksburg with some 30,000 men, retreated beyond Jackson. Grant had determined to get Vicksburg, and he kept to the siege despite enemy and friendly distractions. Confederate efforts to relieve the stronghold Grant parried with fortitude. Attacks from the Northern press, the rumors that eddied congressional halls did more harm. Siege operations were too slow, carpers said; Grant lost too many men to the joint fogs of war and of deep delta country. Lincoln ignored calls for Grant's removal as T. Harry Williams reports (*Lincoln and His Generals,* pp. 272–74). "I rather like the man," he said, because "he doesn't worry and bother me. He isn't shrieking for reinforcements all the time. He takes what troops we can safely give him . . . and does the best he can with what he has. . . ."

In the afterglow of success, Lincoln wrote Grant one of the most graceful confessions ever made by a commander in chief. Writing a week after Vicksburg's surrender, Lincoln said to Grant: "I write this . . . as a grateful acknowledgment for the almost inestimable service you have done the country." As Grant read the letter, he must have seen how much he and the president thought alike about the war. Lincoln said he had watched Grant's operations with growing approval—he had thought Grant should go across the river, march south, recross, and operate below Vicksburg. But he thought that then Grant should have turned south to help General Banks at Port Hudson. "I now wish to make the personal acknowledgment that you were right and I was wrong."

The Vicksburg campaign had opened the Mississippi at a relatively small cost. Since May 1 Grant's casualties came to some 9,500 men.

On Jefferson Davis's side of things, post-Gettysburg analyses were cold indeed. His great hopes for the Department of the West under Joseph E. Johnston had been dashed by the general's incapacity to rise to his powers. Instead of taking charge, ordering armies and supplies where he wanted, taking command of a field army when circumstances dictated, Johnston served more as a coordinator than commander. He knew the Army of Tennessee had lost faith in Bragg and should have removed him. But he felt unable to do that to so staunch a friend of the president's—and he was probably right in his fears. Still, he hewed to old fancies of his own; to him, an army command was the highest post a general could have. And he wanted that more than some amorphous post as facilitator of bits and dribbles. So he missed what was probably the greatest chance of the conflict.

The first week of July, 1863, marked the turning point of the war. The Confederacy had lost not only control of the river, but also a good field army. Combined with Lee's defeat at Gettysburg, the Confederacy, in the first week of July had lost some 50,000 men and 70,000 stands of arms, many of them fine British Enfield rifles. Men and arms were running out in the South. More than that, the Confederacy, cut in twain, now began a precarious dual existence, with Richmond's span of control clearly atrophying. Those twin blows spread gloom across the South, and, combined with the worsening news from Chattanooga, gloom became dread.

Halleck and others, knowing Lincoln's views about the victorious Grant, schemed to get new western hero Meade's command. But Grant, who wanted to keep moving on Mobile, dodged the eastern army. "Whilst I would disobey no order I should beg very hard to be excused before accepting that command," he confessed (quoted in Williams, *Lincoln and His Generals,* p. 275). The Army of the Potomac seemed to wallow in bad luck. Certainly it battled formidable odds and enemies.

William Starke Rosecrans faced lesser obstacles, but acted with greater timidity. Not until June 26, 1863, did he finally move his army from Murfreesboro. Halleck had prodded him restlessly since January. Bragg, his army starved for men as all aid went to Vicksburg, held on below Murfreesboro and kept pressure on the enemy by cavalry raids that earned little—and on one of those, the famed Rebel raider John Hunt Morgan was captured. Rosecrans countered with equally fruitless mounted expeditions.

Bragg's main concern was Chattanooga: he had to hold that strategic city. A rail center that anchored one of the Confederacy's main east-west trunks, Chattanooga also anchored the mountain barrier to Alabama and Georgia. If the Federals took it, they would have interior lines for advancing in almost any direction. When Rosecrans started, he moved with deceptive speed—and he ran Bragg's Kentucky campaign in reverse. Maneuvering instead of fighting, he had by June 30 forced the Rebels back to Tullahoma. Again swift marches almost trapped Bragg north of Elk River. By July 4 Bragg fell back on Chattanooga.

In the woeful news of those first July days, Jefferson Davis understood better than most the strategic portent of Bragg's failure but had little mourning time. Critical blows at Vicksburg and Gettysburg overshadowed the Army of Tennessee's slow agony. With Vicksburg's garrison and important arms supplies gone, Bragg's beleaguered force propped the Confederacy's sagging left shoulder. If that shoulder broke . . . In a way, the fall of Vicksburg unburdened Confederate planning. Most of the time Davis and Seddon had been forced to defend wrong objectives to satisfy local commands—but this time they were right to concentrate on saving a city. Chattanooga's logistical and morale value could not be exaggerated. Even Joe Johnston acted like a theater commander as he sent Bragg some units he had collected near Jackson. He knew Bragg's scant 44,000, including 14,000 cavalry, had to hold several possible Tennessee River crossings against Rosecrans's 65,000. And Grant might reinforce Rosecrans.

A strategic crisis faced Davis's government. Only scattered bodies of men could be stripped from such places as Mobile. Lee showed reluctance to take a western command. What could be done to sustain Bragg? The old idea of detaching Longstreet's corps from Lee's army reappeared. Longstreet was for it; he wanted an independent chance for glory. Lee reluctantly approved; want of men made it about the only workable option, if Bragg were to be quickly strengthened. Bragg's recent call for S. B. Buckner's 9,000-man corps from Knoxville yielded the main rail line from Richmond to Chattanooga. Longstreet's move would have to be made on round-about rail routes. On September 6, Longstreet received his coveted orders. He wanted Bragg's command; victory might win it, if the First Corps could arrive in time.

Bragg's situation had good and bad potential. By the end of August he had virtually forted up in Chattanooga and had deployed

Gen. Nathan Bedford Forrest's cavalry as a screening force along the east bank of the Tennessee. Rosecrans began crossing on August 20 and aimed to sever Bragg's supply line below the city. Bragg's cavalry greatly outnumbered their mounted foes and brought Bragg copious intelligence of enemy moves through various mountain passes south of Chattanooga. News of "rats from so many holes" baffled him, and not until September 8 did he realize the threat to his rear. He evacuated Chattanooga that night – outmaneuvered, he left without a fight. But he planned one.

Victorious and overconfident, Rosecrans stumbled into trouble. Part of it came from ground, the rest from unexpected Rebels. Maps were perennially poor; Rosecrans knew that east of the Tennessee and below Chattanooga various mountains and ridges covered approaches to the city. Cut by various passes and defiles, the ridges were real and puzzling barriers. Bad maps and scarce cavalry left "Rosy" more ignorant of terrain than he guessed.

Bragg had sound strategic sense, once he found out what was happening. He plotted the destruction of the Army of the Cumberland. Rosecrans had split his force into three widely separated units. Bragg, suddenly seized with aggressiveness, concentrated to pick off these exposed units, piecemeal. Everything went wrong with his proposed attack on September 10: Gen. T. C. Hindman failed to move speedily, other subordinates wallowed in timidity, and Rosecrans escaped. He escaped during the next several days. Bragg nearly isolated several Federal forces, but lost them to slow obedience to good orders. He complicated his problem by not being close enough to the front personally to insist on quick action. But he kept to the offensive, never yielding initiative to his opponent.

Longstreet's corps had moved with remarkable speed, despite the long circuit through the deep South. His lead elements, under Gen. John B. Hood, arrived early on September 18, in time to join an attempt to turn the Union left, resting nearly ten miles south of Chattanooga, along Chickamauga Creek. Delays again frustrated Rebel hopes, but more men arrived during the night, and Bragg planned to press on next day. Bitter, confused, and uncertain fighting took up most of September 19, with Bragg really unaware of what happened. He stubbornly held to the attack.

During the night Rosecrans strengthened his line and ordered field works erected on the left. When the Rebels launched their drive at about 9:30 A.M. on September 20, Federal resistance slowed them from the start.

Bragg stuck to his flanking plan and ordered an echelon attack on a close timetable. Early Rebel success against Gen. George H. Thomas on the left prompted Rosecrans to send help from his right. But in sending it, he left a gap in his line that Longstreet exploited expertly late in the morning. Rosecrans's battle went to pieces; some of his men bolted the field. Swept up in the confused retreat himself, Rosecrans did not know of the heroic stand on the left that earned Thomas his battle name: "The Rock of Chickamauga." Thomas finally had to retreat since he was left virtually alone.

Bragg had won, but he failed to pursue, much to Forrest's frustration. As Rosecrans pulled his remnants into Chattanooga, both sides counted Chickamauga's costs. Rosecrans sustained 16,000 casualties out of a force of some 58,000. Bragg, with about 66,000 engaged, lost 18,500 – nearly twenty-eight percent on both sides. Rosecrans lost more than men, of course; he had lost the initiative and huddled in Chattanooga's defenses. Bragg partially surrounded the town and cut Federal supply lines down to one uncertain road. Rosecrans faced starvation as Bragg's men and cannon sat atop such surrounding heights as Missionary Ridge and Lookout Mountain.

Neither commander could boast about Chickamauga. True, Bragg won, but failure to reinforce his attack at crucial times on the twentieth robbed him of the smashing victory he designed. Thomas had saved Rosecrans from the disaster his own tactical errors almost ensured.

Bragg still had the initiative. He could stay where he was and maintain the investment; he could cross the river and flank Rosecrans out of the city and force him to fight; or, he could leave an observation force in front of Rosecrans and move quickly to beat Burnside's small force at Knoxville. His unwonted daring fled; he chose to sit and besiege.

Lincoln read dispatches from Chattanooga in mounting gloom. Since the battle, he thought that Rosecrans had acted "stunned like a duck hit on the head." The president wanted Chattanooga held at all costs – he easily grasped its strategic value – and ordered reinforcements from Meade's idle army. In a sweeping reorganization, Lincoln put all western departments and armies under General Grant. Directing Grant to look at the Chattanooga situation, the president gave him full authority to do whatever seemed best. In effect, he copied Davis's theater command scheme. Grant replaced Rosecrans with Thomas.

Energy, audacity, and courage were Grant's contribution to his new post. Wasting no time, he organized several attacks on Bragg's lines, each time gaining an advantage. Bragg, apparently confident of his lofty lines, had finally detached Longstreet to take Knoxville and had to go on the defensive against Grant. In a dazzling series of attacks, Grant's army unexpectedly carried Bragg's lines at Lookout Mountain on November 24 and smashed through the main front along Missionary Ridge the next day. Grant failed to pursue.

Bragg's army fled to the southeast, leaving some 6,500 casualties behind. Grant's lost about 5,800.

President Davis had reason to regret his earlier decision to overlook criticism by Bragg's generals and keep him in command after the Kentucky campaign. As the Army of Tennessee retreated into northwest Georgia, Davis accepted Bragg's resignation. Despite personal reservations, the president, on December 16, 1863, appointed Joseph E. Johnston to replace Bragg—it was Johnston's proudest moment.

Longstreet failed to take Knoxville. Grant, using the full logistical powers of his new command, sent help to Burnside, which forced the besiegers to abandon their task. Longstreet fell back to Greeneville, Tennessee, where he could either rejoin Lee or threaten Grant's left. His withdrawal signaled the end of the western campaign in 1863, a year that saw Grant win two of the Union's major objectives: control of the Mississippi and possession of Chattanooga, which ensured control of Tennessee and a good route to the heart of Dixie.

Out of the year's turmoil, Grant emerged and Bragg faded. The Union grew stronger in the west, and the Confederacy's power ebbed as the Trans-Mississippi Department went into a kind of semi-independence. Lincoln stated the main import of the western year from the North's standpoint: "The Father of Waters again goes unvexed to the sea" (quoted in James M. McPherson, *Ordeal by Fire*, p. 333).

Jefferson Davis could point to nothing positive from the year in the west save the continued presence of the Army of Tennessee—strange army of lost battles and opportunities; army of rustics led by incompetents, sometimes by fools; army that still survived and fought and bled and lost and stayed to its steadfast duty.

CHAPTER ELEVEN

Into the Wilderness
and an Awful Killing Summer

Great armies have souls of their own, a character molded by fiery trial and awful error, a temper trued for lasting. As with the Army of Tennessee, so, too, the Union Army of the Potomac. Unlucky army, legend said, badly officered and slackly run, army of wasted lives and chances, army cast against the fates and Lee.

Still, it stood bulwark to Washington. The ranks had about abandoned hope of leaders when they lost McClellan, and events had not disabused their whimsy. Meade, though, had fought them well and had a kind of following. Quickly he learned the army's ways, and after Gettysburg, like all of Lee's opponents, he had settled the army into rebuilding and refitting. And the army appreciated that—"getting after Lee" had never been a winning game. Waiting to throw him back had always been best. Meade clearly agreed.

Halleck and Lincoln wanted something done in those post-battle days, with Longstreet absent and Lee's army licking wounds. But Meade had the stubbornness of his predecessors. He needed men, supplies, horses before he could move. That sloth cost him men. Despairing of an offensive against Lee, Lincoln had ordered the detachment of some of Meade's army to Rosecrans, and Lee tried to take advantage of a weakened opponent.

In early October, 1863, the Army of Northern Virginia crossed the Rapidan, in a familiar try to get around Meade's right and move on Washington. Meade, despite the detachments, largely outnumbered Lee, but the old Napoleonic flanking threat made him retreat. Lee saw his chance: he would hit Meade's retreating columns at Bristoe Station, break them up, take their trains, and give battle on the old Manassas grounds. It did not happen. Lee's command structure had lost its nimbleness; orders went slowly, were even more slowly obeyed. The Army of Northern Virginia showed alarming signs of attrition at almost every level. None marked the import more clearly than Lee.

Both armies found no opportunity to strike a decisive blow, and the Rebels retired. Meade picked up the gauntlet, as good weather held in Virginia. Halleck and Lincoln hazed him into crossing the Rapidan with about 85,000 men on November 26, 1863, in a campaign to turn Lee's right. Meade, much to Lincoln's chagrin, still aimed at Richmond, not at Lee's army; he hoped to maneuver Lee into a retreat to his capital. With slightly less than 50,000 men – Longstreet had not yet returned – Lee quickly moved to meet the enemy and occupied strong positions along Mine Run. So strong were Lee's works that Meade found no point of attack; his campaign failed aborning.

Operations along Mine Run confirmed a new element shaping battles: field entrenchments. Wherever armies halted, they now threw up heavy works – even the Rebs, who hated digging. It should have happened earlier, considering the engineering background of all West Pointers. For the early Civil War years, though, marching and stand-up fighting were the ways of American combat. Grady McWhiney and Perry D. Jamieson, in *Attack and Die: Civil War Military Tactics and the Southern Heritage* (1982), suggest that this passion for massed attacks reflected the Celtic element in both armies, especially the Southern armies. Whatever the cause, discretion overcame foolish valor. Improved weapons brought a fearsome growth in firepower. Massed rifles and vastly improved field artillery shattered old European attack formations. Immense slaughter forced entrenching. Field works sprang up on western battlefields earlier than in Virginia – but by winter, 1863, veteran troops were deft diggers.

They were also superior scavengers, especially Lee's men. Virginia

Artillery, like this mortar in place at Petersburg, dominated the Civil War in a new way. Standing in front next to it are Col. H. L. Pratt and Gen. H. J. Hunt, chief of artillery.

had been picked clean for three years by various hordes. Fervent efforts by commissary and quartermaster agents to supply the Army of Northern Virginia during the cold winter of 1863–64 produced starvation rations. The men foraged a bare landscape. Lee constantly urged supplies in letters increasingly like Washington's missives from Valley Forge. Davis gave all he could, but scarcity crippled the logistical chain. By mid-1863 effects of attrition spread widely across the Confederacy.

Attrition in the South affected not only manpower but also facilities and transportation. With repeated drives to fill ranks, some supply officers and men were shifted and often replaced by the less skilled and able-bodied. Shortages of shops and equipment retarded repair of war-worn trains and tracks. Rickety wagons, patched harness, thinned horses and mules became standard equipment by mid-1863 –all symptoms of scarcity. Sometimes these symptoms came from maladministration. Bad planning occasionally piled up supplies at one point, while starving another. Coordination came hard to a government harassed by states' rights dogma. War pressure finally led Davis's government to limited nationalization of transportation, an essential policy, though damned as dictatorial.

Men were in shortest supply. The Confederacy's military population was running out. Various schemes had been tried to fill the ranks: amnesty for deserters, bounties, special leave consideration; but as the war ground on, morale sagged and even a slight wound became a discharge. Congressmen understood the manpower crisis and two years earlier had passed the first draft law in American history on April 16, 1862. Approved by most state courts, often opposed by such ardent states' rights governors as Georgia's Joseph E. Brown and North Carolina's Zebulon B. Vance, the act produced too few men. Congressmen responded with increasingly stiff draft acts; they even attacked the sacrosanct substitution system, expanded eligible years from seventeen to fifty, and cut exemptions. Slaves were enrolled for work on fortifications; too late in the war, they were accepted as soldiers–a few actually donned the gray just at the end.

In the government's view, conscription's special value came from its control of the national manpower pool. Under war department regulations, the war secretary could manage the Confederacy's work force, put men where they could best serve the cause. Without the draft, though, Rebel ranks would probably have disintegrated by the end of 1862. Modern estimates indicate some 82,000 conscripts enrolled east of the Mississippi from April 16, 1862, until war's end.

All these efforts reflected attrition's pressure on a beleaguered land.

But even with vast manpower superiority, the United States had had difficulty in keeping up its armies. War's early glamor quickly tarnished; volunteers soon wrote brothers to avoid camps as places of pestilence, vermin, and corruption. Religious youths were horrified at the army's coarse secular tone. Patriotism became a selective thing. After Lincoln's first call for volunteers, a visible drop in response had prompted the so-called draft of 1862. A mishmash of state and national programs, this early conscription effort kept responsibility at the state level; where states had no laws drafting the militia, national orders were to prevail. Liberal exemptions and a general lack of enthusiasm vitiated these early efforts. Not until March 3, 1863, did the United States congress adopt conscription. Enforcement wallowed in problems. New York City—where Mayor Fernando Wood supported the South—writhed in draft riots July 13–15, and resistance sparked across the North, from rural Vermont (where a thousand Irish quarry workers rampaged) to Boston to Saint Paul, Minnesota. Chicago's raucous Third Ward—infamously called The Patch—saw more than four thousand men, women, and children obstruct draft officials, then attack police who tried to keep order.

As in the South, control of national manpower ranked as an important result of Northern conscription. Additions to the ranks, though, were vital to the Federal cause. Best estimates are that some 249,259 men were drafted and that 86,724 paid to be exempted—consequently 162,535 men actually were drafted. Federal numbers were swelled in July, 1862, by the acceptance of blacks in the ranks. Almost 180,000 served in many regiments during the war.

Conscription's value to both sides came more from suasion than from force. Simply because a draft law lurked in the background, volunteering and re-enlistments continued.

As cold clamped on the armies' camps at the end of 1863, mere existence took precedence over war. But beyond the armies, the Union basked in a kind of boom in economy and in spirit—although inflation dented the boom a bit. Laborers complained of exploitation, and their efforts at organization produced little. Still, although real wages declined somewhat, conditions were better because the country recognized labor's value. Wartime entertainments flourished across the North, with resident and traveling troupes performing patriotic tableaux and standard classics to large audiences. Theaters charmed with stagy, often terrible charades of quick Union victory over wicked slavocrats, especially in the early days when many basked in a war that might bring discipline to a materialistic people.

As the conflict lengthened and became a revolution in everything, plays and diversions seemed hardly enough. The pace of things accelerated; new ideas, machines, tools, methods, learning, death stretched the strength of everyone. Even though the country seemed humming with energy and gorging on expansion, casualty lists ran a roll of dread in almost every household. Pundits might praise the nation's morale, but too much was happening too fast. A kind of neurosis stalked the land, created new ailments—"irritable heart" was one that afflicted young recruits—and one noted physician saw war

Black troops under Gen. Edward Ferrero at Petersburg, June, 1864

as triggering neurasthenia. The widespread use of morphine in field medicine created a special problem for veterans and families already shattered by loss: morphine addiction.

Lincoln's sensitivity tuned him to his country's worries. And he guessed the fragility of national purpose in wake of so much sacrifice to such small reward. He did cosmetic things to show energy and boost resolve. As a new campaign season approached, the president reshaped his entire command structure. After years of groping, he recognized in Grant the general he had looked for to run the war. On March 10, 1864, the president promoted Grant—who was forty-one years old—to the revived rank of lieutenant-general and made him general in chief of the Union's armies. More than half a million men were in Grant's charge—he could hardly handle the heavy minutiae of so many and happily accepted Lincoln's notion that Halleck be chief of staff to handle relations between a civilian president and his general and between the general and his various department commanders. This arrangement, as T. Harry Williams observed in *Lincoln and His Generals* (1952), signaled the beginning of a modern command system.

Grant knew his headquarters had to be close to Washington but did not want to stay in the city. He went to the field with the Army of the Potomac. Meade remained in command, but Grant's tent always stood close by. This potentially volatile arrangement worked well, because both generals cooperated. Grant gave overall strategic directions and left tactics to Meade. As a result, an aggressive spirit permeated the army as it began to believe in victory.

The new general in chief shared President Lincoln's understanding of power and pressure. He knew the United States had vastly more war resources than the Confederacy and worked to use that superiority. As Winfield Scott had proposed much earlier and Lincoln had often repeated, Grant wanted to put as many troops in the field as possible and press the Confederates everywhere—a program that T. Harry Williams has called Operation Crusher. Recognizing that uncoordinated Federal operations permitted the enemy to shift troops from one army to another on inner lines, Grant intended to put all Federal forces into some kind of action.

Grant projected three major offensives for the 1864 campaign. The Army of the Potomac under Meade (whom Grant came to admire greatly) would stick to Lee's army and not let go, while smaller forces would threaten Richmond from the James River side and the Shenandoah Valley. A big western army under one of Grant's favorites, William T. Sherman, would press the Army of Tennessee through north Georgia, into Atlanta. While pressing Joe Johnston, Sherman would also destroy Southern war resources in the state. As Sherman moved south, an army under Gen. N. P. Banks would march from New Orleans to Mobile, whence it might link with Sherman and at last secure one of Grant's pet objectives, the Chattanooga-Mobile line.

These good plans quickly skewed. Banks started an expedition of his own up the Red River in Louisiana in April. Using gunboats, he hoped to capture Shreveport, headquarters of the Trans-Mississippi Department, and bring war to Texas. Everything went wrong. He lost the major battle of Mansfield on April 8, 1864, had to abandon his campaign, and was unable to make the Mobile move. An infuriated Grant wanted Banks removed, but Lincoln needed that general's considerable political support in the upcoming election. He put Banks on the shelf at New Orleans.

Sherman continued to get his army of more than 90,000 ready to move against Johnston, and Meade collected more than 100,000 to hurl against Lee. These coordinated offensives would stress the Confederacy at its weakest point: manpower. Unable to shift troops from one army to the other, the Davis administration would have to scrape the barrel for men. This situation put a premium on killing in the coming campaigns, for the North had replacements aplenty while the South had few.

Anxious but not despondent, Davis, too, had modified his command structure. He brought the unemployed Bragg to Richmond as his chief of staff—an absurdity in the eyes of Bragg's widening circle of critics. But Davis had a point: Bragg might not have a taste for fighting, but he did have some strategic sense. Davis would have preferred advice from Lee on all Confederate fronts, but Lee's attention fixed on Meade. Bragg, at least, knew logistical fundamentals and the odd ways of Rebel soldiers.

After that key appointment, President Davis rejoiced in Banks's failure and in the limited successes of Bedford Forrest at Okolona, Mississippi, and also of Gen. Joseph Finegan's victory over a Federal expedition into Florida's interior (the Battle of Olustee) in late February, 1864. Glad of some good news, the Confederate president had done valiantly in sending help to both Johnston and Lee—Johnston received men from Alabama and Mississippi and the coast until he counted nearly 60,000 and Lee, supported again by Longstreet's corps, counted almost 70,000. Despite the heavy threat hanging over the Confederacy, the new year had promise. If Sherman and Grant (Meade) could be checked, the coming Union election might make George McClellan president and change the character of the war. Another Union stalemate might finally induce foreign recognition.

Meade advanced just after midnight on Wednesday, May 4, 1864, and so began a desperate series of battles in the Virginia Wilderness, near the old Chancellorsville fields. Fearsome fighting on May 6 found Lee going forward to encourage his men and hearing them cry, "Lee to the rear! General Lee to the rear!" Longstreet took a serious wound as carnage among generals shook command. Oppor-

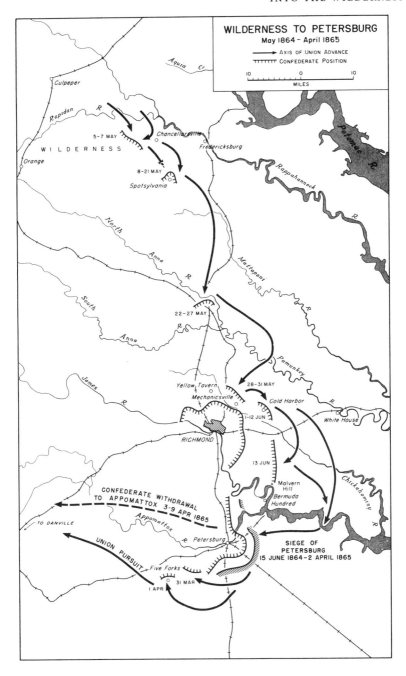

WILDERNESS TO PETERSBURG
May 1864 - April 1865

→ AXIS OF UNION ADVANCE
⊤⊤⊤⊤⊤⊤ CONFEDERATE POSITION

10   0   10
MILES

Aquia Cr.

Culpeper

Rapidan R.

WILDERNESS

Orange

5-7 MAY   Chancellorsville
           Fredericksburg

8-21 MAY

Spotsylvania

Potomac R.

Rappahannock R.

North Anna R.

Mattapont R.

South Anna R.

James R.

22-27 MAY

Pamunkey

Yellow Tavern
Mechanicsville   28-31 MAY
                  Cold Harbor

White House

1-12 JUN

RICHMOND

13 JUN

Chickahominy R.

CONFEDERATE WITHDRAWAL
TO APPOMATTOX 3-9 APR 1865

Malvern
Hill
Bermuda
Hundred

TO DANVILLE

Appomattox R. Petersburg

UNION PURSUIT

Five Forks

1 APR   31 MAR

SIEGE OF
PETERSBURG
15 JUNE 1864-2 APRIL 1865

tunities came to both sides, were seized and missed, and light field works proved their value. By the end of the day, opposing lines were stabilized. More than 100,000 Federals were in the fight, and 17,666 of them were casualties. Across from them, Lee lost 7,500 from his 60,000 engaged. Unlike his predecessors, Meade did not turn back to Washington. Grant, holding the strategic initiative, ordered continued pressure on the Rebel right. Lee hurried troops to intercept the enemy at Spotsylvania Court House–an important road hub.

Running into unexpected Rebel entrenchments at the Court House on May 8, Meade's men were repulsed, and fighting faded. Grant ordered Gen. Philip Sheridan to take the cavalry on a raid to hit Lee's communications and so divert Stuart's riders. Light encounters next day underscored a general field readjustment and further entrenching. Gen. John Sedgwick, one of Meade's corps commanders, fell. Meade ordered a morning attack.

A general assault on Rebel works in late afternoon, May 10, was repulsed, but some dents were made at cost. Light skirmishing took up most of the next day, and Grant determined to exploit a salient in Lee's works by a major attack on May 12. Furious assaults and counterattacks occupied the day. Gen. Richard S. Ewell's corps of Lee's army lost some 4,000 prisoners in before-dawn fighting. "The Bloody Angle" consumed men for most of the afternoon and into the night. This day ranks as one of the costliest of the war: Federal casualties ran to 6,800; Confederate to 5,000 killed and wounded. All the rage and fury cost men and gained little–but attrition stalked Lee's ranks. Not until May 18 did the Wilderness again see hard war. That day a series of Union attacks against strengthened Rebel works failed. So strong were the enemy lines at Spotsylvania that Grant decided to shift the battle farther to Lee's right.

Actions around the Court House cost more than 17,500 Federal casualties out of a force of 110,000. Confederate losses were much less but not really known. In the Wilderness and Spotsylvania engagements together, Meade lost 33,000 men–a terrible price for slow success.

Lee guessed Grant's moves and also turned toward the southeast. Some good news came from the James River front. Beauregard, brought up to command in southern Virginia, had pretty well bottled up Gen. Benjamin F. Butler's army at Bermuda Hundred Neck. Richmond's situation need not worry Lee for the moment.

He worried about Grant. Along the North Anna River confused

Dead Confederates at Spotsylvania. One of the Union soldiers viewing the bodies holds a sprig of flowers.

fighting won Lee a chance to hit a divided Federal army. Lee was sick, subordinates confused, and the opportunity passed. By May 26, Grant ordered another flank move, far to Lee's right, but Rebels got to Cold Harbor first and began a maze of fortifications. On June 1 and 2 Meade's men concentrated at Cold Harbor. Many bluecoats, seeing the awesome strength of Lee's trenches, wrote their names on slips of papers and pinned them on their uniforms to avoid being listed among the unknown. Meade attacked at 4:30 A.M. in a pell-mell rush to smash through Lee's lines. Three Union corps stormed toward Rebel works and in a little over half an hour were repulsed at probably the highest cost of any day in the war. Numbers are disputed, but Union losses are put between 7,000 and 12,000 to 1,500 Confederates. Lee remarked that at the height of the action the concentrated Confederate rifle fire sounded like wet sheets tearing in the wind.

Grant's stubborn campaign raised high criticism at home. One prominent Northerner (Charles Francis Adams, Jr., quoted in Long, *Civil War Day by Day,* p. 515) rightly wrote that the Army of the Potomac "has literally marched in blood and agony from the Rapidan to the James." At last Grant halted. So strong were opposing entrenchments that neither side could attack. Grant was of different stuff than McClellan and the others—he would not quit. What would he do and where?

Being closer to Richmond gave Lee logistical advantages. As he had fallen back on his base, he received some reinforcements and reorganized. Beauregard's situation grew bothersome, though, since Butler outnumbered him two to one. Nonetheless, Lee hoped Beauregard could put some men in front of Richmond, between the James and the Chickahominy.

Sticking to the scheme of pressing Lee from various quarters, Grant engineered several incursions into Virginia. One, led by Gen. David Hunter, would probe the upper end of the Shenandoah, take Staunton, destroy crops and shops, pin down scattered Confederate forces, and perhaps force Lee to detach forces to stop him. Hunter's threat came after Lee had brought Gen. John C. Breckinridge's small force from the valley to help fill the Cold Harbor lines. With Sheridan's cavalry on the way to Hunter, Lee sent Breckinridge back—but his 2,100 men seemed a hollow threat to Hunter's 18,000. Breckinridge and Lee guessed Lynchburg as Hunter's objective—a supply center vital to Lee. Something would have to be done about Hunter.

Desperately short of men, eager to avoid a siege of the capital or its consort city, Petersburg, some thirty miles south, Lee knew that any further detachments from his ranks would commit him to the heavy works ringing Richmond. But he had to act and so sent Jubal Early to deal with Hunter. It seemed a good choice. Early commanded Jackson's old Second Corps, including remnants of the Army of the Valley, had drive and gall and liked fighting. Lee gave him wide discretion.

Early dealt with Hunter at Lynchburg, then moved boldly down the Shenandoah to threaten Harper's Ferry, crossed the Potomac, and moved directly on Washington. Only the stubborn defense of the Monocacy River in Maryland by Gen. Lew Wallace (of *Ben Hur* fame) prevented Early's 12,000 from possibly wandering the streets of Washington. Early's raid in June and July, 1864, was in the best offensive-defensive tradition. Lee hoped it would force Grant to send troops to protect the Union capital; it did, but not enough to change the odds compounding at Richmond and Petersburg. At its high point, Early's campaign reached the outskirts of Washington – even fired on President Lincoln in a Yankee redoubt! – and convinced the *London Times* that "the Confederacy is more formidable as an enemy than ever." Which proved, at least, that ruses sometimes work. The raid had scared Lincoln and Halleck and cleared the valley of Federals at a crucial time. Early remained a threat as Lee left him there to protect the granary of the army.

By the end of the first week in June, Lincoln and Grant were disappointed. Grant, who intended to fight on to Richmond "if it . . . [took] all summer," found that it would take that time and more. After all the carnage, his campaign had failed. True, he was seven miles from Richmond, but Lee's army remained intact. No good way seemed open to flank the Rebs away from Richmond's formidable entrenchments. Grant told the president he intended to give up the direct approach, cross south of the James, and hit Richmond from its supposedly soft underbelly. He wanted to get Lee out in the open for a decisive blow. Lee would not come out of his lines to fight Grant's battle, hence he magnified his numbers.

But Grant, for once, fooled the wily Rebel leader. He began crossing the James on June 12, and Lee lost him for several days. Expecting a move south of the James, Lee struggled for definite information of Grant's movements. A large part of the Army of the Potomac crossed beyond the river, and by June 15, 16,000 Yankees attempted to attack Beauregard's 3,000 men defending Petersburg. Bad maps, combined with botched orders and short rations, confused the advance, and Beauregard's brilliant countermeasures staved off ruin.

If Lee was confused about Grant's whereabouts, Beauregard was not – he kept reporting mounting Union numbers to Lee, kept asking for help. Lee remained unconvinced of Grant's doings. Beauregard held against mounting numbers, contracted his lines, stripped his Bermuda Hundred line, and by June 17 had done about all he could do to hold Petersburg. That day Lee sent heavy reinforcements and saved the southern gateway to Richmond.

The four-day defense of Petersburg had been bloody—Meade lost about 8,000 killed and wounded. Confederate losses were less, but unaffordable. On June 8, 1864, the siege of Petersburg began. Over the next nine months Lee's lines would extend some thirty miles and be held by scarcely more than 60,000 men against Meade's 110,000.

Jefferson Davis, like Lincoln, wondered how much more of woe Confederates could take. There was more to the country than Yankees wanted to admit, or than modern students will allow. The fact of the existing armies told a lot about public war support. But spirit sagged, no doubt about it. "Bread riots" had erupted in Richmond and other major centers—riots brought on by shortages and by skyrocketing prices the poor could not pay. Theaters were jammed with people looking for escape. Confederate music and songs—good barometers to feelings in a sentimental land—ran now to dirges and dismal lyrics of longing and loss: "Lorena," "I Am a Rebel Soldier, and Far from My Home." Probably "The Southern Soldier Boy" best caught the growing grief of a nation:

> Young as the youngest who donned the gray.
>   True as the truest who wore it,
> Brave as the bravest he marched away,
>   Hot tears on the cheeks of his mother lay.
> Triumphant waved our flag one day,
>   He fell in the front before it.
>
> CHORUS:
> A grave in the wood with grass o'ergrown,
> A grave in the heart of his mother,
> His clay in the one, lifeless and lone,
> But his memory lives in the other.

Grant's men thronged the southern gateway to Richmond—and if Lincoln believed armies alone were the proper targets of campaigns, Davis and his countrymen knew the value of their capital. To lose Richmond would be catastrophic. All sinews of a shrinking land strained to keep that city. Even a factious congress—made more so by the 1863 elections that returned an anti-Davis majority—recognized disaster pending in March, 1865, and, after doubling its own pay, hastened to enact all the hard war measures Davis had long urged. Stiffer excess profits taxes on corporations and individuals were levied, along with a draconian value added tax on all taxed items; stiffer penalties greeted desertion; railroads were put under direct control of the secretary of war—Davis had his way in the foredawn of doom.

As Sherman thrust toward interior Georgia, waves of refugees swayed in front of him, clogging roads and towns; their tales of terror bought a new element to war. Industries, laboratories, supply agencies suffered and moved with the people, when possible—a sea change in the body social. There was a Confederacy still, but one with Federals in the heartland, one sickened and in spasm.

CHAPTER TWELVE

On to History

Although many Northerners thought Grant's new strategy had failed, it was working. While Meade battled his way through northern Virginia, Sherman moved from Chattanooga against the Army of Tennessee. As both Lee and Johnston called for men, Davis and Seddon found fewer and fewer; the pool of eligible white males had about gone dry. Some brigades were scraped together in the spring and summer of 1864. They came from outlying posts and stations, usually from exposed coastal areas, and each shipment brought loud plaints from fearful governors.

Large sections of the Southern heartland had no men left. Part of the manpower problem stemmed from the need to protect the armies' lines of communication against Union raiders, even against disaffected Southerners and organized deserters. When such hard war measures as conscription and impressment drained patriotism, trouble sprang up behind the lines, and Confederate troops were detached for rear area security. As summer fighting ground on, casualties could not be replaced. Grant's suspension of prisoner exchange in April, 1864, hit the South harder than the North–there were more than

150,000 Johnny Rebs in Union prisons who were badly needed in the ranks.

All the logistical support network of the Confederacy frayed under Grant's joint offensives. Ammunition and clothing could be had, but distribution to the armies became problematical as Federal cavalry wrecked railroads and bridges. Rations grew thinner as agricultural areas went to the enemy. An iron shortage crippled cannon production, while scarcity of copper cut percussion cap manufacture. Civilian food supplies shrank as well. Indispensable things began to vanish from Southern homelife. Leather, of course, was almost an artifact by 1864; cloth grew scarce. Worst of all, salt, essential to meat preservation, grew scarcer as Federal forces sought out mines and desalinization sites along the coastline. Taken separately, these deprivations were slight; added to invasion, they were devastating.

Across the South symptoms of sagging morale could be seen, not only in death, shortages of food and clothing and everyday things, but also in the growing numbers of refugees who trekked a piteous pathway toward safety, somewhere. Diaries of these dispossessed tell harrowing tales of hasty departure from homesteads, of often chilly reception by communities too poor for hospitality. There were shining moments of real welcome, too, to offset the dreariness of a squatter's life. "Cold water parties" took the place of customed conviviality. Relatives seeking kinfolk in safer climes were often a special wartime trial to be borne with family decency. Refugees reinforced the lack of everything. Where they came, they consumed: food, clothing, such money as there was, medicines.

Medicines touched a poignant need in every community, every home. Since the North branded chloroform, other narcotics, and most remedies as "contraband of war," anesthetics were scarce, and surgery soothed mainly by whisky; treatment of all ailments relied on old-time folk nostrums or Indian cures. Cruel enough for soldiers, vengeful and inhumane for children. Resentment rose to anger over such Yankee animus, but the drabness, the losses, the apparently endless war twisted anger slowly into defeatism.

Nor was the North immune. Hard campaigns ground up Union manpower as well. As the staggering summer casualty lists filled Northern papers, a great spasm of agony and anger racked the country. Lincoln, like Grant, was hotly criticized, so much so that Lincoln thought he might lose the election of 1864, might not even get the Republican nomination. He would stay the course, but his opponent might not. The cause might be lost by ballots. Signs of war weariness and apathy multiplied.

No signs of defeatism showed in the field. Hope and determination fired Sherman's 100,000 men, divided into three armies, as they began moving on May 7, 1864. Sherman launched a great raid, aimed at smashing Johnston's army and at cutting Georgia in two with a sixty-mile-wide incursion to the sea; it became a surprisingly effective logistical campaign that threatened key Confederate arsenals, armories, and depots. The first rush stalled, though, for Johnston's lines were too strong.

Johnston always had a good eye for ground, and he had entrenched his 60,000 devoted men along a ridge near Dalton, Georgia. Sherman tried turning the Confederate left. Johnston began one of history's great retreats. Grudgingly, he backed down the Western and Atlantic Railroad toward Atlanta, entrenching where he could, standing when he had a chance to fight, slipping away from flankers with sure control of his men and a baffling sense of timing. The retreat became a kind of offense; Sherman repeatedly deployed, skirmished, flanked, only to see Johnston's rear guard still ahead. Resaca, Cassville, the Etowah River each stalled Sherman's march. At Kennesaw Mountain, June 27, 1864, Johnston bloodily repulsed a major attack.

To a worried Lincoln, Sherman's operations offered vast potential. If Johnston's army were destroyed, Lee would be finished quickly—the war would end. But by the end of June, Sherman seemed to be emulating Grant's tactics—pushing the enemy back on his base while extending Federal supply lines. At last Johnston fell back into Atlanta's strong defenses and awaited battle.

Through the weeks of Johnston's retreat President Davis watched in mounting frustration. How far would he go? When would he fight? Where? These understandable presidential questions Johnston either ignored or parried with some excuse about security. Silence might have been prudent because Johnston would have had to say that the army took precedence over cities or ground and he would keep it between Sherman and the sea. Still, the president had a right to know what the commander of one of the South's main armies had in mind.

When Johnston pulled his men into the Atlanta lines, Davis made a mistake. Unable to find out what his general planned, save retreat, the president replaced him with Gen. John Bell Hood, one of Lee's best division leaders and a corps commander in the Army of Ten-

Joseph E. Johnston

nessee. The army seethed because the men loved Old Joe and many felt that Hood had undermined him and frustrated chances to attack Sherman. There was truth to the thought, but the deed stood, and fear chilled veterans who had so often been pawns to ambition.

Davis had asked Lee's advice and heard cautionary words about leaving a good man in command—words, too, about Hood being a fighter but perhaps not quite of army command caliber. Hood knew that Davis wanted a fight for Atlanta. Two hard attacks failed, and Hood abandoned the city on September 2, 1864. This disaster crowned a grinding summer for the South. Atlanta's fall proved the value of

William T. Sherman

Grant's Operation Crusher. Sherman wasted no time as he prepared a march through the industrial heart of Georgia and on to the coast, finally on to Charleston–the Cradle of Secession.

Hood made a good attempt to recoup his fortunes. Guessing that a march up Sherman's communications toward Nashville would force him to follow, Hood started for Tennessee in November. Sherman followed only a short way, left Hood to others, and marched on to the sea. Hood wasted the flower of his army in a useless frontal attack at Franklin, then limped on to clamp a partial siege on Nashville. Gen. George Thomas, the Rock of Chickamauga, broke the siege on December 15–16, 1864, and also broke Hood's army.

Bits and pieces of it drifted back to Georgia, where Johnston tried to rebuild it as some kind of buffer to Sherman. Out from Sherman's army had gone clouds of "bummers," who burned, pillaged, degraded young and old as they carried freedom's flag, they thought, in that year of Jubilo. A gallant remnant of the Army of Tennessee won a partial victory at Bentonville and was finally surrendered to Sherman at Durham Station, North Carolina, on April 26, 1865.

Robert E. Lee hated the defensive. As siege lines snaked ever longer south and west along the Appomattox River, as more of his men were confined in burgeoning labyrinths of trenches, he knew the initiative had firmly passed to Grant. Now the Army of Northern Virginia faced the daily routine of attrition–the slow death Lee had so fiercely fended. Petersburg had to be held: important rail lines joined there from the deep South that sustained the army's thin rations and supplies. Federal cavalry raided the lines, and others coming directly to Richmond, but Fitzhugh Lee–who took over from the dead Jeb Stuart–kept them at bay, even though his horsemen had to forage almost forty miles from the Confederate Army. Supplies grew fewer as enemy thrusts into the logistical heart of the Confederacy sapped resources. Rickety trains ran slower, more unreliably as winter dug the army deeper into its strange dirt warrens.

From mid-June, 1864, to April 2, 1865, the siege distracted Lee. Desperately he wanted to maneuver, to get out and attack Grant with some chance of flanking him, turning him back toward the Potomac. Grimly Grant stuck to his trenching, steadily extending westward to thin out Lee's defenders. These long months saw raids and frontal assaults, charges, skirmishes, and the endless, dreary burrowing. Occasionally the lines twitched. A Union attempt to blow up part of the Rebel trenches, the Battle of the Crater on July 30, 1864,

Ulysses S. Grant during the Wilderness campaign, 1864

Robert E. Lee, 1865, after the war

Abandoned Richmond in ruins; the armory in the foreground

changed veteran Rebel feelings of respectful animosity into ones of real bitterness against black troops, who gallantly led the way into an inferno. Lee several times during the winter of 1864–65 tried to gain a strategic advantage along the trench lines – but heavy Union strength in men and guns usually prevailed.

Lincoln guessed at the stresses wracking the Confederacy. He condoned a personal peace mission to Richmond by Frank Blair, which brought agreement from Jefferson Davis to talk peace – against his better judgment. He thought the North would deny Confederate independence, and that was nonnegotiable. On February 3, 1865, three Confederate commissioners, including Vice-President Stephens, met with Lincoln and William H. Seward aboard a steamer at Hampton Roads. Lincoln talked generously about easy peace terms; he seemed willing to negotiate anything save disruption of the Union. So this hope ended as Davis had expected.

Davis tried one more foreign gamble, despite all previous disappointments. He believed the South would agree to anything save subjugation and so sent Louisianian Duncan F. Kenner to Britain with a question: would Britain grant recognition in exchange for emancipation. If so, the slaves would go free, a pledge he had no constitutional authority to make, but he believed, with Lincoln, that victory would exonerate him. Too late, said British authorities; emancipation had already happened. Victory rested where it always had – on the Rebs with Lee and Johnston.

At Petersburg, Grant slowly moved to his left until Lee's 45,000 men were stretched to cover nearly thirty miles of line. Caught in the geometry of a closing circle, Lee, who had been made commander in chief of the Confederate armies in February, 1865, by a congress angry at Davis, planned a desperate gamble. If, somehow, he could cripple Grant's army, he would leave a holding force at Petersburg and join Johnston to defeat Sherman. The combined Confederate armies would then return to deal with Grant. The plan had the forlorn logic of fantasy, but Lee tried. At 4:00 P.M., March 25, 1865, he launched an attack on Fort Stedman at the north end of the Union lines. This costly failure – 5,000 casualties – was seen by an encouraged President Lincoln. Grant followed that battle with a major effort on Lee's attenuated right and on April 2, 1865, the Confederate line broke. Lee evacuated Petersburg and Richmond and began marching southwestward in hope of finding rations, and perhaps of joining Joe Johnston.

On April 9, 1865, with Federal columns front and rear, Lee went to the house of Wilmer McLean (who had moved when the first Battle of Bull Run overran his residence) at Appomattox Court House and surrendered the Army of Northern Virginia. Terms were generous. Horsemen kept their horses, officers their side arms, the men got Union rations, everyone was paroled on Grant's authority. Like the Confederacy itself, Lee's army had been first exhausted, then defeated.

With Lee's surrender, the remaining Confederate fragments yielded everywhere, and by the last of May the first of the modern wars was over. The last errant Confederate banner came down when the CSS *Shenandoah* struck her colors at Liverpool on November 6, 1865.

The Confederacy went on to legend and the United States to world power.

CHAPTER THIRTEEN

What Kind of War?

What kind of war had ended? It had begun as an old-fashioned war of armies against armies and had evolved, as Bruce Catton observed, into a "war against. . . ." Building its own momentum, it had become a great rolling change agent that freed the slaves, that reworked social, economic, and political seams, and that left America forever different.

It had been a war of more than 10,500 fights. It had also been the first war of the Industrial Revolution, of machinery and firepower and engineering beyond imaginings – a war of railroads and iron ships and submarines and rifled cannon, of telegraphs and rudimentary air observation, of massed firepower and the end of massed charges, of machines against gallantry. And the costs had been commensurate with new machinery and with new ways of killing.

Estimates vary, but adjusted statistics reported by Long (*Civil War Day by Day*, pp. 704, 708–11) indicated 110,100 Union killed and mortally wounded, 224,580 dead of disease, plus 275,175 wounded and 30,192 prisoner of war dead – for 640,047 total casualties of all causes. Confederate figures are more conjectural (no naval figures are available), but a fair assessment gives 94,000 Confederates killed or mortally

178

wounded, 164,000 dead of disease, plus 194,026 wounded and from 26,000 to 31,000 prisoner of war dead – for 483,026 total casualties of all causes. Total Civil War deaths from all causes are estimated at least at 653,872, with minimum wounded totals at 469,201, for an overall war casualty figure of 1,123,073. More than twenty-five percent of the 1861 available manpower of the North and South became casualties of some kind. Note the Southern proportional imbalance.

Numbers alone do not tell the whole wages of the war. Vast areas of the South stood scorched, ravaged, pillaged, wrecked by friendly and hostile armies. And in both North and South the returning veterans were not the men they had been. A dread scythe of maiming and disfiguring passed across their ranks; whole men of war were hard to find. Lame, broken, and blind lingered as mutant hostages of conflict.

Numbers do offer interpretive aid in assessing the monetary costs of America's great war. Again, figures are disputed, but careful students estimate that Northern costs ran to about thirteen billion dollars and that Southern costs could hardly have been less than six billion dollars.

There were, of course, intangible horrors to count in hope, pride, courage, and faith, which affected psyches, North and South, for generations to the present. In that terrible expense of blood and treasure and intangibles, Americans tested whether they had the courage of their convictions in democracy.

Two revolutions had happened. The Northern revolution ushered in a period of restless boom and expansionism virtually unimagined before the war. The revolution in war and in management and banking and especially in the triumph of pragmatism reworked the Union – despite war's human and material cost – into a place not only of plenty but also of certainty in progress.

War destroyed the Old South. Davis's revolution provided the methods and means to carry the Confederacy on beyond its resources into utter exhaustion and nearly utter devastation. His revolution changed the South from the richest to the poorest part of the Union, even while it gave the South a stronger sense of unity than it had had before the war. But these were the effects of losing a war, not the measure of the revolution itself.

The real revolution in the South was partly the result of Davis's success and partly a result of his defeat. From his success in making war and creating a political structure to support it came familiarity with centralization that prepared the South to accept–down the road, when the memories of war had faded a bit–a single national industrial system with a strong social and political infrastructure. From his ultimate failure came the abandonment, save in sentimental terms, of a dream of a different democracy embraced in Southern independence.

The war means differently to both sections. Northerners read of it and view it on television as a terrible episode in history, but without much sense of presence. Some Southerners console their haunt of wasted gallantry with the myth of a Lost Cause.

Out of the crucible of carnage came confirmation that all men were forever free and the Union was indivisible, that the Lost Cause was forever lost. This confirmation reforged old themes of brotherhood into a new and stronger America. There were scars and sorrows and anguish mixed in a strange, surging thirst for destiny.

The Civil War was really the War of American unification.

Bibliographic Essay

Books on the Civil War flood libraries and bookstores. Useful in threading through the tangle of titles is Allan Nevins, James I. Robertson, Jr., and Bell I. Wiley, *Civil War Books: A Critical Bibliography*, 2 vols. (Baton Rouge: Louisiana State University Press, 1967–69). Other important bibliographies include Paolo E. Coletta, *A Bibliography of American Naval History* (Annapolis: Naval Institute Press, 1981), and the peerless listing of Civil War sources in J. G. Randall and David Herbert Donald, *The Civil War and Reconstruction* (2nd ed., Lexington, Mass.: D. C. Heath, 1969), which still stands as the most comprehensive single-volume treatment of the subject.

Invaluable for information on Civil War archival materials are Henry Putney Beers, *The Confederacy: A Guide to the Archives of the Government of the Confederate States of America* (1968; new ed., Washington, D.C.: National Archives and Records Administration, 1986); and Kenneth W. Munden and Henry P. Beers, *The Union: A Guide to Federal Archives Relating to the Civil War* (1962; new ed., Washington, D.C.: National Archives and Records Administration, 1986). See also James C. Neagles's *Confederate Research Sources: a Guide to Archive Collections* (Salt Lake City, Utah: Ancestry Pub., 1986).

Maps are essential to any study of the Civil War; there are many sources and types. The following collections are especially helpful: *The Official Atlas of the Civil War* (originally titled *Atlas to Accompany the Official Records of the Union and Confederate Armies* (1891–95; new edition: New York: T. Yoseloff, 1958); Vincent J. Esposito, ed., *The West Point Atlas of American Wars*, 2 vols. (New York: Praeger, 1959); Matthew F. Steele, *American Campaigns*, 2 vols. (Washington, D.C.: B. S. Adams, 1909); *A Guide to Civil War Maps in the National Archives* (Washington, D.C.: National Archives, 1986); Richard W. Stephenson, comp., *Civil War Maps: An Annotated List of Maps and Atlases in the Library of Congress* (Washington, D.C.: Library of Congress, 1989). Joseph B. Mitchell, *Decisive Battles of the Civil War* (New York: Putnam, 1955), designs his maps to follow modern highways through the battlefields. The best modern survey of Civil War battlefields is Frances H. Kennedy, ed., *The Civil War Battlefield Guide* (Boston: Houghton, Mifflin, 1990).

Particularly helpful are several compendiums of miscellaneous and important data: Mark Mayo Boatner III, *The Civil War Dictionary* (New York: D. McKay Co., 1959); E. B. Long, with Barbara Long, *The Civil War Day by Day: An Almanac, 1861–1865* (Garden City, N.Y.: Doubleday, 1971), an essential book for Civil War study and especially for many of the battle statistics cited in this book; H. S. Commager, ed., *Documents of American History*, 2 vols. (New York: Appleton-Century-Crofts, 1949 [5th ed.]), and *The Blue and the Gray: The Story of the Civil War as Told by Participants*, 2 vols. (Indianapolis: Bobbs-Merrill, 1950); Jon L. Wakelyn, ed., *Biographical Dictionary of the Confederacy* (Westport, Conn.: Greenwood Press, 1977); C. E. Dornbusch, comp., *Regimental Publications and Personal Narratives of the Civil War: A Checklist*, 3 vols. (New York: New York Public Library, 1961–71).

Government publications from both sides are invaluable. The best general sources on the conflict are *The War of the Rebellion: A Compilation of the Official Records of the Union and Confederate Armies*, 70 vols. in 127 and index (Washington, D.C.: Government Printing Office, 1880–1901), which also boasts an important volume of maps; and *Official Records of the Union and Confederate Navies in the War of the Rebellion*, 30 vols. and index (Washington, D.C.: Government Printing Office, 1894–1927). A helpful tool to use with the army records is Frederick Dyer, *A Compendium of the War of the Rebellion*, 3 vols. (1908; new ed., New York: T. Yoseloff, 1959). Northern congressional debates are presented in the *Congressional Globe;* of equal usefulness— though of a kind to defy listing— are the "Congressional Documents," indexed in Benjamin P. Poore, *Descriptive Catalogue of Government Publications, 1774–1881* (Washington, D.C.: Government Printing Office, 1953), along with the *United States Statutes at Large* (serial; Washington, D.C.: Government Printing Office, 1872). For overall use of the voluminous government publications, see Anne M. Boyd, *United States Government Publications* (3rd ed., New York: Wilson, 1949); and L. F. Schmeckebier, *Government Publications and Their Use* (1936; 2nd rev. ed., Washington, D.C.: Brookings Institution, 1969).

Confederate official publications are enormously helpful. The legislative history of laws can be traced in the *Journal of the Congress of the Confederate States of America,* 7 vols. (Washington, D.C.: Government Printing Office, 1904–1905), as well as in the "Proceedings of the Confederate Congress, reprinted from Richmond newspapers, edited by Frank E. Vandiver, *Southern Historical Society Papers* 12 (1953) and 13–14 (1959). For laws and resolutions, see James M. Matthews, ed., *The Statutes at Large of the Provisional Government of the Confederate States of America,* (Richmond: R. M. Smith, 1864; reprinted, Buffalo, N.Y.: William S. Hein, 1988), and *The Statutes at Large of the Confederate States of America,* 5 vols. (Richmond, Va.: R. M. Smith, Printer to the Congress, 1862–64); along with Charles W. Ramsdell, ed., *Laws and Joint Resolutions of the Last Session of the Confederate Congress (November 7, 1864–March 18, 1865) Together with the Secret Acts of Previous Congresses* (Durham, N.C.: Duke University Press, 1941).

Photographic collections on the Civil War are many, and most of them good. Matthew Brady set a tone of coverage unmatched since his era; his colleagues on both sides preserved for all time the peculiar freshness and agony of a brother's war. First among collections, not only because it was the first, but also because of scope, concept, and textual explanation, is Francis T. Miller, *The Photographic History of the Civil War,* 10 vols. (New York: Review of Reviews Co., 1911). Especially good because of Bruce Catton's text, is Richard M. Ketchum, ed., *The American Heritage Picture History of the Civil War* (New York: American Heritage Publishing Company, 1960). David Donald provides the narrative for a splendid collection by Hirst D. Milhollen and Milton Kaplan, eds., *Divided We Fought: A Pictorial History of the War, 1861–1865* (New York: MacMillan, 1956). Among the most recent collections, one that offers excellent essays on major topics, along with many previously unseen pictures, is William C. Davis, ed., *The Image of War, 1861–1865,* 6 vols. (Garden City, N.Y.: Doubleday, 1981–84); see also his *Touched by Fire: A Photographic Portrait of the Civil War,* 2 vols. (Boston: Little, Brown, 1985–86). For a special look at Confederate sea operations, see Philip Van Doren Stern, *The Confederate Navy: A Pictorial History* (Garden City, N.Y.: Doubleday, 1962). A relatively recent volume on Lincoln shows the special usefulness of popular prints: Harold Holzer, Gabor Borritt, and Mark E. Neely, Jr., *The Lincoln Image: Abraham Lincoln and the Popular Print* (New York: Scribner Press, 1984).

The Public Broadcasting System's 1990 presentation of Ken Burns's television series *The Civil War* gave a unique evocation of the war through montages and movement and background music. That series also inspired a fine companion volume, by Geoffrey C. Ward, with Ric Burns and Ken Burns, *The Civil War: An Illustrated History* (New York: Knopf, 1990).

General histories of the Civil War increase annually. James Ford Rhodes, *History of the United States from the Compromise of 1850 to the McKinley-Bryan Campaign of 1896*, 8 vols. (New York: MacMillan Company, 1892–1922), remains a classic. Comprehensive and insightful is the superior series by Allan Nevins: *Ordeal of the Union*, 2 vols. (1849–57; New York: Scribner, 1947), *The Emergence of Lincoln*, 2 vols. (1857–61; New York: Scribner, 1950), *The War for the Union*, 4 vols. (New York: Scribner, 1959–71). Randall and Donald, *The Civil War and Reconstruction*, cited earlier, offer a balanced analysis of the war and its aftermath.

Two valuable one-volume surveys are by British scholars: William R. Brock, *Conflict and Transformation: The United States, 1844–1877* (New York: Penguin, 1973); and Peter J. Parish, *The American Civil War* (New York: Holmes & Meier, 1975). Important American views are contained in David M. Potter, *Division and the Stresses of Reunion, 1845–1876* (Glenview, Ill.: Scott, Foresman & Company, 1973); David Herbert Donald, *Liberty and Union* (Boston: Little, Brown & Company, 1978); Emory M. Thomas, *The American War and Peace, 1860–1877* (Englewood Cliffs, N.J.: Prentice-Hall, 1973). James M. McPherson has written two sound and stirring histories, *Ordeal by Fire: The Civil War and Reconstruction* (New York: Knopf, 1982), and *Battle Cry of Freedom: The Civil War Era* (New York: Oxford University Press, 1988). Bruce Catton, *The Centennial History of the Civil War*, 3 vols. (Garden City, N.Y.: Doubleday, 1961–65), presents a highly readable analysis by a mature scholar. Shelby Foote, *The Civil War, A Narrative*, 3 vols. (New York: Random House, 1958–74), is narrative history at its best. Raimondo Luraghi, *Storia della Guerra Civile Americana* (Turin: G. Einaudi, 1966), is an outstanding one-volume history by a distinguished Italian student of the Civil War. Charles P. Roland, *An American Iliad: The Story of the Civil War* (Lexington: University Press of Kentucky, 1991), offers a splendid synthesis that combines military narrative with shrewd political, economic, and social assessments.

Of special importance, considering the thesis of revolutions in this book, are Emory M. Thomas, *The Confederacy as a Revolutionary Experience* (Englewood Cliffs, N.J.: Prentice-Hall, 1971); Bell I. Wiley,

Road to Appomattox (New York: Atheneum, 1968); Paul D. Escott, *After Secession: Jefferson Davis and the Failure of Confederate Nationalism* (Baton Rouge: Louisiana State University Press, 1978); Drew Gilpin Faust, *Creation of Confederate Nationalism: Ideology and Identity in the Civil War South* (Baton Rouge: Louisiana State University Press, 1988); James M. McPherson, *Abraham Lincoln and the Second American Revolution* (New York: Oxford University Press, 1990). Phillip S. Paludan, *"A People's Contest": The Union and Civil War, 1861–1865* (New York: Harper & Row, 1988), is a superior book, a splendid survey of the North at war that shows the changes wrought by conflict. Charles Royster, *The Destructive War* (New York: Alfred A. Knopf, 1991), examines the growing anger generated by the war. Important indications of anti-abolition sentiment in the North can be found in Bernard Mandel, *Labor, Free and Slave: Workingmen and the Anti-Slavery Movement in the United States* (New York: Associated Authors, 1955); and in Madeline H. Rice, *American Catholic Opinion in the Slavery Controversy* (New York: Columbia University Press, 1944). See also Robert Leckie, *None Died in Vain* (New York: Harper Collins, 1990).

A comprehensive look at wartime changes in the Confederacy can be found in the best nonmilitary history of the South at war, E. Merton Coulter, *The Confederate States of America, 1861–1865* (Baton Rouge: Louisiana University Press, 1950). A new view of Confederate financial failure is contained in Douglas B. Ball, *Financial Failure and Confederate Defeat* (Urbana: University of Illinois Press, 1991). Most helpful in looking at medicine in war are Horace H. Cunningham, *Doctors in Gray: The Confederate Medical Service* (Baton Rouge: Louisiana State University Press, 1960), and his *Field Medical Services at the Battles of Manassas* (Athens: University of Georgia Press, 1968); George W. Adams, *Doctors in Blue* (New York: H. Schuman, 1952); and George W. Smith, *Medicines for the Union Army* (Madison, Wis.: American Institute of the History of Pharmacy, 1962). William Q. Maxwell, *Lincoln's Fifth Wheel* (New York: Longmans, Green, 1956), treats the Sanitary Commission in detail.

War's impact on Northern thought is weighed in George Frederickson, *The Inner Civil War: Northern Intellectuals and the Crisis of Disunion* (New York: Harper & Row, 1965). War's effect on literature is assessed in Daniel Aaron, *The Unwritten War: American Writers and the Civil War* (New York: Knopf, 1973); in Edmund Wilson's stimulating *Patriotic Gore: Studies in the Literature of the American Civil War* (New York: Oxford University Press, 1962); in F. O. Matthiessen,

American Renaissance: Art and Expression in the Age of Emerson and Whitman (New York: Oxford University Press, 1941); and in R. W. B. Lewis, *The American Adam: Innocence, Tragedy and Tradition in the Nineteenth Century* (Chicago: University of Chicago Press, 1958).

Essential in judging Southern morale are three books by Richard B. Harwell: *The Brief Candle: The Confederate Theatre* (Mercer, Ga.: Mercer University Press, 1971), *Confederate Music* (Chapel Hill: University of North Carolina Press, 1950), and *Songs of the Confederacy* (New York: Broadcast Music, 1951); one by Drew Gilpin Faust, *The Creation of Confederate Nationalism,* cited earlier; and one by James W. Silver, *Confederate Morale and Church Propaganda* (Tuscaloosa, Ala.: Confederate Publishing Company, 1957). Vital to an understanding of the mind of the Southern leader class are C. Vann Woodward, ed., *Mary Chesnut's Civil War* (New Haven: Yale University Press, 1981); and Robert M. Myers, ed., *The Children of Pride: A True Story of Georgia and the Civil War* (New Haven: Yale University Press, 1972).

Essential to the story of Union and Confederate foreign policy are David P. Crook, *The North, the South, and the Powers* (New York: Wiley, 1974); Norman A. Graebner, "Northern Diplomacy and European Neutrality," in David Herbert Donald, ed., *Why the North Won the Civil War* (Baton Rouge: Louisiana State University Press, 1960); Lynn M. Case and W. F. Spencer, *The United States and France: Civil War Diplomacy* (Philadelphia: University of Pennsylvania Press, 1970); Frank J. Merli, *Great Britain and the Confederate Navy, 1861–1865* (Bloomington: Indiana University Press, 1970): Frank A. Jenkins, *Britain and the War for the Union,* 2 vols. (Montreal: McGill-Queen's University Press, 1974–80); Karl Marx and Friedrich Engels, *The Civil War in the United States,* ed. Richard Enmale (New York: International Publishers, 1937). Frank L. Owsley, *King Cotton Diplomacy: Foreign Relations of the Confederate States of America* (1931; 2nd ed. rev. by Harriet C. Owsley, Chicago: University of Chicago Press, 1959), still stands as the best treatment of Confederate diplomacy.

Causes of the war engage students constantly. In addition to the general works listed, see Thomas J. Pressly, *Americans Interpret Their Civil War* (Princeton: Princeton University Press, 1954), for an overall look. See especially William L. Barney, *The Road to Secession: A New Perspective on the Old South* (New York: Praeger, 1972); William Catton and Bruce Catton, *Two Roads to Sumter* (New York: McGraw Hill, 1963); Daniel W. Crofts, *Reluctant Confederates: Upper South Unionists in the Secession Crisis* (Chapel Hill: University of North

Carolina Press, 1989); Richard Current, *Lincoln and the First Shot* (Philadelphia: Lippincott, 1963); William Freehling, *Prelude to Civil War: The Nullification Controversy in South Carolina* (New York: Harper & Row, 1966), and *The Road to Disunion: Secessionists at Bay, 1776–1854* (New York: Oxford University Press, 1990); C. C. Goen, *Broken Churches, Broken Nation: Denominational Schisms and the Coming of the American Civil War* (Macon, Ga.: Mercer University Press, 1985); Michael F. Holt, *The Political Crisis of the 1850s* (New York: Wiley, 1978); James L. Huston, *The Panic of 1857 and the Coming of the Civil War* (Baton Rouge: Louisiana State University Press, 1987); John McCardell, *The Idea of a Southern Nation: Southern Nationalists and Southern Nationalism, 1830–1860* (New York: Norton, 1979); Stephen B. Oates, *To Purge This Land With Blood: A Biography of John Brown* (New York: Harper & Row, 1970); Richard H. Sewell, *A House Divided: Sectionalism and Civil War, 1848–1865* (Baltimore: Johns Hopkins University Press, 1988); Ralph A. Wooster, *The Secession Conventions of the South* (Princeton: Princeton University Press, 1962), and *The People in Power: Courthouse and Statehouse in the Lower South, 1850–1860* (Knoxville: University of Tennessee Press, 1969).

Important in the whole discussion is Kenneth M. Stampp, *And the War Came: The North and the Secession Crisis, 1860–61* (Baton Rouge: Louisiana State University Press, 1950), and *The Causes of the Civil War* (Englewood Cliffs, N.J.: Prentice-Hall, 1965); David M. Potter, *The Impending Crisis, 1848–1861* (New York: Harper & Row, 1976); Avery O. Craven, *The Growth of Southern Nationalism, 1848–1861* (Baton Rouge: Louisiana State University Press and Littlefield Fund for Southern History [Austin, Texas], 1953); Donald E. Reynolds, *Editors Make War: Southern Newspapers in the Secession Crisis* (Nashville: Vanderbilt University Press, 1970).

State secession studies abound. Most useful among recent ones are William L. Barney, *The Secessionist Impulse: Alabama and Mississippi in 1860* (Princeton: Princeton University Press, 1974); Walter L. Buenger, *Secession and the Union in Texas* (Austin: University of Texas Press, 1984); Steven A. Channing, *Crisis of Fear: Secession in South Carolina* (New York: Simon & Schuster, 1970); Michael P. Johnson, *Toward a Patriarchal Republic: The Secession of Georgia* (Baton Rouge: Louisiana State University Press, 1977); Marc W. Kruman, *Parties and Politics in North Carolina, 1836–1865* (Baton Rouge: Louisiana State University Press, 1983); James M. Woods, *Rebellion and Realignment: Arkansas's Road to Secession* (Fayetteville: University of Arkansas, 1987).

For slavery as a cause of the conflict, see U. B. Phillips, *American Negro Slavery* (New York: D. Appleton, 1918), which is the classic non-repressive interpretation of the slavery system; opposed to Phillips is Kenneth M. Stampp, *The Peculiar Institution* (New York: Knopf, 1956), which shows slavery as hurtful to the slaves.

Stanley Elkins, *Slavery: A Problem in American Institutional and Intellectual Life* (3rd ed., Chicago: University of Chicago Press, 1976), focuses on the personality changes wrought by the slave system; that book generated many replies, among which are Ann J. Lane, ed., *The Debate over Slavery: Stanley Elkins and His Critics* (Urbana: University of Illinois Press, 1971); and John W. Blassingame, *The Slave Community: Plantation Life in the Antebellum South* (New York: Oxford University Press, 1979). Also of importance in slave studies are Richard C. Wade, *Slavery in the Cities* (New York: Oxford University Press, 1964); Robert S. Starobin, *Industrial Slavery in the Old South* (New York: Oxford University Press, 1970); and Eugene D. Genovese, *Roll, Jordan, Roll: The World the Slaves Made* (New York: Pantheon Books, 1974). A neglected but highly intriguing study of causation and the war is Carl Russell Fish, *The American Civil War: An Interpretation,* ed. W. M. Smith (New York: Longmans, Green, & Company, 1937).

Theories of war and tactical applications are covered in J. F. C. Fuller, "The Place of the American Civil War in the Evolution of War," in *Army Quarterly* 26 (1933); Edward Hagerman, *The American Civil War and the Origins of Modern Warfare* (Bloomington: Indiana University Press, 1988), which also includes incisive views on logistics; Karl von Clausewitz, *On War* (1831; Princeton: Princeton University Press, 1976); Henry W. Halleck, *Elements of Military Art and Science* (1846; Westport, Conn.: Greenwood Press, 1971); William J. Hardee, *Rifle and Infantry Tactics,* 2 vols. (Philadelphia: Lippincott, Grambo & Company, 1855); Antoine Henri de Jomini, *The Art of War* (1838; Westport, Conn.: Greenwood Press, 1971); Dennis Hart Mahan, *An Elementary Treatise on Advanced-Guard, Outpost, and Detachment Service of Troops* (1847; New Orleans: Bloomfield & Steel, 1861; commonly referred to simply as *Outpost*); Grady McWhiney and Perry D. Jamieson, *Attack and Die: Civil War Military Tactics and the Southern Heritage* (University, Ala.: University of Alabama Press, 1982); Russell F. Weigley, *History of the United States Army* (New York: Macmillan, 1967). See also, *Regulations, CSA* (1861–64), and *Regulations for the Army of the United States* (serial; Washington, D.C.: Government Printing Office, 1857, 1861, 1863).

Strategic considerations are the subject of Archer Jones, *Confederate Strategy from Shiloh to Vicksburg* (Baton Rouge: Louisiana State University Press, 1961), and "Jomini and the Strategy of the American Civil War, a Reinterpretation," in *Military Affairs* 34 (1970); T. L. Connelly and Archer Jones, *The Politics of Command: Factions and Ideas in Confederate Strategy* (Baton Rouge: Louisiana State University Press, 1973); John G. Moore, "Mobilization and Strategy in the Civil War," in *Military Affairs* 24 (1960); Archer Jones, *The Art of War in the Western World* (Urbana: University of Illinois Press, 1987), pp. 409–18, which offers an intriguing analysis.

Byzantine problems of organization are covered in Fred A. Shannon, *The Organization and Administration of the Union Army, 1861–1865*, 2 vols. (1928; Gloucester, Mass.: P. Smith, 1965); A. H. Meneely, *The War Department, 1861* (New York: Columbia University Press, 1928); Frank E. Vandiver, *Rebel Brass: The Confederate Command System* (Baton Rouge: Louisiana State University Press, 1956).

Biographies exist for major war figures and for many minor ones. Begin with a look for memoirs or reminiscences, which are numerous and amazingly revealing on both sides. Most important leaders arranged their memories of the war, and the literature is vast. For a highly selective selection of works on Lincoln see: James G. Randall, *Lincoln the President*, 4 vols., the last vol. by Richard Current (New York: Dodd, Mead, 1945–55); Benjamin Thomas, *Abraham Lincoln: A Biography* (New York: Knopf, 1952). Also good is Reinhard H. Luthin, *The Real Abraham Lincoln* (Englewood Cliffs, N.J.: Prentice-Hall, 1960). Stephen B. Oates, *With Malice toward None: The Life of Abraham Lincoln* (New York: Harper & Row, 1977), is colorful but controversial. The classic, but highly uncritical work, is Carl Sandburg, *Abraham Lincoln: The Prairie Years*, 2 vols. (New York: Harcourt, Brace, 1926), and *Abraham Lincoln: The War Years*, 4 vols. (New York: Harcourt, Brace, 1939). Important collections of Lincoln papers exist, in addition to the usual presidential compilations. See especially Roy P. Basler and others, eds., *The Collected Works of Abraham Lincoln*, 9 vols. (New Brunswick, N.J.: Rutgers University Press, 1953–55).

Helpful on phases of Lincoln's career are David M. Potter, *Lincoln and His Party in the Secession Crisis* (New Haven: Yale University Press, 1942); David Herbert Donald, *Lincoln Reconsidered: Essays on the Civil War* (New York: Knopf, 1956). See also Richard Current, *Lincoln and the First Shot* (Philadelphia: Lippincott, 1963); Earl S. Miers, ed., *Lin-*

coln Day by Day, 3 vols. (Washington, D.C.: Lincoln Sesquicentennial Commission, 1960); J. G. Randall, *Lincoln, the Liberal Statesman* (New York: Dodd, Mead, 1947); Norman A. Graebner, ed., *The Enduring Lincoln* (Urbana: University of Illinois Press, 1959). In addition, for special phases of Lincoln as president, see Burton J. Hendrick, *Lincoln's War Cabinet* (Boston: Little, Brown & Company, 1946); Harry J. Carman and Reinhard H. Luthin, *Lincoln and the Patronage* (New York: Columbia University Press, 1943); William B. Hesseltine, *Lincoln and the War Governors* (New York: Knopf, 1948); T. Harry Williams, *Lincoln and the Radicals* (Madison: University of Wisconsin Press, 1941). Essential to a study of Lincoln and the war powers are J. G. Randall, *Constitutional Problems under Lincoln* (Urbana: University of Illinois Press, 1951); and George F. Milton, *Lincoln and the Fifth Column* (New York: Vanguard Press, 1942). Extremely important in the area of constitutional history is Harold M. Hyman, *A More Perfect Union: The Impact of the Civil War and Reconstruction on the Constitution* (New York: Knopf, 1973).

Lincoln as commander-in-chief is best covered in T. Harry Williams, *Lincoln and His Generals* (New York: Knopf, 1952); and Colin R. Ballard, *The Military Genius of Abraham Lincoln: An Essay* (1926; 1st American ed., Cleveland: World Publishing Company, 1952). Kenneth P. Williams, *Lincoln Finds a General: A Military Study of the Civil War,* 5 vols. (New York: MacMillan, 1950–59), is also helpful on this subject.

Jefferson Davis is almost a historical stepchild, hardly given a loser's mite. He lacks a good biography, though several are currently underway. William E. Dodd, *Jefferson Davis* (Philadelphia: G. W. Jacobs & Company, 1907), is still useful, as is Allen Tate, *Jefferson Davis, His Rise and Fall* (New York: Minton, Balch & Company, 1929). Recent studies include Hudson Strode's adulatory *Jefferson Davis,* 3 vols. (New York: Harcourt, Brace, 1955–64); and Clement Eaton's good *Jefferson Davis* (New York: Freedom Press, 1977). The best biography so far is the latest: William C. Davis, *Jefferson Davis: The Man and His Hour* (New York: Freedom Press, 1977).

Davis wrote an important memoir, *The Rise and Fall of the Confederate Government,* 2 vols. (New York: D. Appleton, 1881), which presented his own assessment of the Civil War. Much about him can be found in the biography by his wife, Varina Howell Davis, *Jefferson Davis, Ex-President of the Confederate States of America: A Memoir by His Wife,* 2 vols. (New York: Belford Company, 1890). See, too, Herman M. Hattaway, "Jefferson Davis and the Historians," in Roman J.

Heleniak and Lawrence L. Hewitt, eds., *The Confederate High Command and Related Topics–The 1988 Deep Delta Civil War Symposium: Themes in Honor of T. Harry Williams* (Shippensburg, Pa.: White Mane Publishing Company, 1990); and Frank E. Vandiver, *Their Tattered Flags: The Epic of the Confederacy* (New York: Harper's Magazine Press, 1970).

Collected papers of Davis appear in Dunbar Rowland, ed., *Jefferson Davis, Constitutionalist: His Letters, Papers, and Speeches,* 10 vols. (Jackson: Mississippi Department of Archives and History, 1923). A modern and critical edition of Davis's papers is currently in publication and complete through the first year of the Civil War: Haskell M. Monroe, Jr., James T. McIntosh, Lynda L. Crist, Mary S. Dix, and Richard E. Beringer, eds., *The Papers of Jefferson Davis,* 7 vols. to date (Baton Rouge: Louisiana State University Press 1971–). Important phases of Davis's wartime career are covered, along with activities of his cabinet, in Rembert W. Patrick, *Jefferson Davis and His Cabinet* (Baton Rouge: Louisiana State University Press, 1944). Davis's relations with his commanders have received recent attention in Steven E. Woodworth, *Jefferson Davis and His Generals: The Failure of Confederate Command in the West* (Lawrence: University Press of Kansas, 1990).

Lincoln's "permanent" secretary of War, Edwin M. Stanton, is brilliantly treated in Benjamin P. Thomas and Harold M. Hyman, *Stanton: The Life and Times of Lincoln's Secretary of War* (New York: Knopf, 1962); for Lincoln's navy chief, see John Niven, *Gideon Welles: Lincoln's Secretary of the Navy* (New York: Oxford University Press, 1973); and see Welles's *Diary of Gideon Welles: Secretary of the Navy under Lincoln and Johnson,* 3 vols. (New York: Houghton Mifflin Company, 1911).

General U. S. Grant is the subject of many books. The best biography, also the most recent, is William S. McFeely, *Grant: A Biography* (New York: Norton, 1981). The general's own memoirs rank among the finest military reminiscences of any era, *Personal Memoirs of U. S. Grant,* 2 vols. (New York: Webster, 1885). For an incisive look at Grant's grasp of politico-military matters, see Brooks D. Simpson, *Let Us Have Peace: Ulysses S. Grant and the Politics of War and Reconstruction, 1861–1868* (Chapel Hill: University of North Carolina Press, 1991). A modern edition of Grant's papers is currently appearing under the skillful editorship of John Y. Simon, *The Papers of Ulysses S. Grant,* 18 vols. to date (Carbondale and Edwardsville: Southern Illinois University Press, 1967–). Douglas S. Freeman, *R. E. Lee: A Biog-*

raphy, 4 vols. (New York: Scribner, 1934–35), is an American classic and, combined with his *Lee's Lieutenants,* 3 vols. (New York: C. Scribner's Sons, 1942–44), offers an unmatched portrait of one of the major Civil War leaders. Also useful are Frederick Maurice, *Robert E. Lee, the Soldier* (London: Constable, 1925); and Clifford Dowdey, *Lee* (New York: Bonanza Books, 1965). For nontraditional views of Lee, see Thomas L. Connelly, *The Marble Man: Robert E. Lee and His Image in American Society* (New York: Alfred A. Knopf, 1977), and Alan T. Nolan, *Lee Considered: General Robert E. Lee and Civil War History* (Chapel Hill: University of North Carolina Press, 1991). Grant and Lee are interestingly contrasted in J. F. C. Fuller, *Grant and Lee: A Study in Personality and Generalship* (Bloomington: Indiana University Press, 1957, rev. 1982).

Henry Halleck's wartime contributions are well treated in Stephen E. Ambrose, *Halleck: Lincoln's Chief of Staff* (Baton Rouge: Louisiana State University Press, 1962). George B. McClellan's checkered career is covered in W. W. Hassler, *General George B. McClellan: Shield of the Union* (Baton Rouge: Louisiana State University Press, 1957); and in Stephen W. Sears, *George B. McClellan: The Young Napoleon* (New York: Ticknor & Fields, 1988).

Important aspects of Northern command are revealed in Benjamin P. Poore, *The Life and Public Services of Ambrose E. Burnside, Soldier, Citizen, Statesman* (Providence: J. A. & R. A. Reid, 1882); Walter H. Hebert, *Fighting Joe Hooker* (Indianapolis: Bobbs-Merrill, 1944); Freeman Cleaves, *Rock of Chickamauga: The Life of General George H. Thomas* (Norman: University of Oklahoma Press, 1948); and *Meade of Gettysburg* (Norman: University of Oklahoma Press, 1960). See also Meade, *The Life and Letters of George Gordon Meade, Major General United States Army,* 2 vols. (New York: C. Scribner's Sons, 1913); William M. Lamers, *The Edge of Glory: A Biography of General William S. Rosecrans* (New York: Harcourt, Brace, 1961). For William T. Sherman, see B. H. Liddell Hart, *Sherman: Soldier, Realist, American* (New York: Dodd, Mead, 1929); Lloyd Lewis, *Sherman, Fighting Prophet* (New York: Harcourt, Brace, 1932); J. M. Merrill, *William Tecumseh Sherman* (Chicago: Rand McNally, 1971); and the general's own *Memoirs of General W. T. Sherman,* 2 vols. (New York: D. Appleton, 1875; Library of America edition, 1990). Union logistical problems are probed in the memoirs of the Union's genius of railroads, Herman Haupt, *Reminiscences* (Milwaukee, Wis.: Wright & Joys Company, 1901); Russell F. Weigley, *Quartermaster-General of the Union Army: A Biography of Montgomery C.*

Meigs (New York: Columbia University Press, 1959); and in Thomas Weber, *Northern Railroads in the Civil War, 1861–1865* (New York: King's Crown Press, 1952).

Standard studies of Confederate leaders include T. Harry Williams, *P. G. T. Beauregard: Napoleon in Gray* (Baton Rouge: Louisiana State University Press, 1955); and Beauregard's memoirs in Alfred Roman, *The Military Operations of General Beauregard in the War Between the States, 1861–1865,* 2 vols. (New York: Harper Brothers, 1884); Eli Evans, *Judah P. Benjamin, the Jewish Confederate* (New York: Free Press, 1988); Grady McWhiney, *Braxton Bragg and Confederate Defeat,* vol. 1 (New York: Columbia University Press, 1969), and vol. 2, written by Judith Lee Hallock (Tuscaloosa: University of Alabama Press, 1991); Don Seitz, *Braxton Bragg: General of the Confederacy* (Columbia, S.C.: State Company, 1924); Millard K. Bushong, *Old Jube: A Biography of General Jubal A. Early* (Boyce, Va.: Carr Publishing Company, 1955); and Early's memoirs, *War Memoirs: Autobiographical Sketch and Narrative of the War Between the States,* ed. Frank E. Vandiver (Bloomington: Indiana University Press, 1960).

Also, James I. Robertson, Jr., *General A. P. Hill: The Story of a Confederate Warrior* (New York: Random House, 1987); John P. Dyer, *The Gallant Hood* (Indianapolis: Bobbs-Merrill, 1950); Richard M. McMurry, *John Bell Hood and the War for Southern Independence* (Lexington: University Press of Kentucky, 1982); and Hood's memoirs, Richard N. Current, ed., *Advance and Retreat* (Bloomington: University of Indiana Press, 1959); G. F. R. Henderson, *Stonewall Jackson and the American Civil War,* 2 vols. (1919; London: Longmans, Green & Company, 1936); Frank E. Vandiver, *Mighty Stonewall* (New York: McGraw-Hill, 1957); Charles P. Roland, *Albert Sidney Johnston: Soldier of Three Republics* (Austin: University of Texas Press, 1964); Gilbert Govan and J. W. Livingood, *A Different Valor: The Story of General Joseph E. Johnston, C.S.A.* (New York: Bobbs-Merrill, 1956); and Johnston's memoirs, *Narrative of Military Operations Directed During the Late War Between the States,* ed. Frank E. Vandiver (Bloomington: Indiana University Press, 1959); D. B. Sanger and T. R. Hay, *James Longstreet* (Baton Rouge: Louisiana State University Press, 1952); William G. Piston, *Lee's Tarnished Lieutenant: James Longstreet and His Place in Southern History* (Athens: University of Georgia Press, 1987).

Also, Emory M. Thomas, *Bold Dragoon: The Life of J. E. B. Stuart* (New York: Harper & Row, 1986); Joseph T. Durkin, *Stephen R. Mallory: Confederate Navy Chief* (Chapel Hill: University of North Carolina Press, 1954); H. Allen Gosnell, *Rebel Raider: Being an Account of Raphael Semmes' Cruise in the C.S.S. Sumter* (Chapel Hill: University of North Carolina Press, 1948); W. Adolphe Roberts, *Semmes of the Alabama* (Indianapolis: Bobbs-Merrill, 1938); Joseph H. Parks, *General Edmund Kirby Smith, C.S.A.* (Baton Rouge: Louisiana State University Press, 1954).

Alexander H. Stephens, controversial vice-president of the Confederacy, has been the subject of too little scholarly attention, but see Rudolph von Abele, *Alexander H. Stephens: A Biography* (New York: Knopf, 1946); and Stephens's own, *A Constitutional View of the Late War Between the States: Its Causes, Character, Conduct and Results*, 2 vols. (Philadelphia: National Publishing Company, 1868–70).

Encyclopedic biographies of generals in both armies are given in Ezra J. Warner, *Generals in Gray: Lives of the Confederate Commanders* (Baton Rouge: Louisiana State University Press, 1959), and *Generals in Blue: Lives of the Union Commanders* (Baton Rouge: Louisiana State University Press, 1964).

General military histories of the Civil War are too numerous to list. Among the most readable, as well as reliable, are Michael C. C. Adams, *Our Masters, the Rebels: A Speculation on Union Military Failure in the East, 1861–1865* (Cambridge: Harvard University Press, 1978); R. Ernest Dupuy and Trevor N. Dupuy, *The Compact History of the Civil War* (New York: Hawthorn, 1960); Thomas E. Griess, ed., *The American Civil War* (Wayne, N.J.: Avery Publishing Group, 1987); Herman Hattaway and Archer Jones, *How the North Won: A Military History of the Civil War* (Urbana: University of Illinois Press, 1983); Allan Nevins, *The War for the Union,* cited earlier.

Important studies of the North and South at war touch heavily on military matters. See, for instance, Bruce Catton, *This Hallowed Ground* (Garden City, N.Y.: Doubleday, 1956); Emory M. Thomas, *The Confederate Nation: 1861–1865* (New York: Harper & Row, 1979); Frank E. Vandiver, *Their Tattered Flags: The Epic of the Confederacy,* cited earlier.

Campaign studies are legion. Some campaigns are best covered in biographies of contending leaders, such as McClellan, Pope, Lee, Jackson, Bragg, Grant, and Halleck. Outstanding among those works touching specifically on campaigns are John Bigelow's classic, *The Campaign of Chancellorsville* (New Haven: Yale University Press, 1910); Edwin B. Coddington, *The Gettysburg Campaign: A Study in Command* (New York: C. Scribner's Sons, 1968), which should be used with

George R. Stewart's *Pickett's Charge: A Microhistory of the Final Attack at Gettysburg* (Boston: Houghton Mifflin, 1959), and with Frank A. Haskell's moving personal evocation, edited by Bruce Catton, *The Battle of Gettysburg* (Boston: Houghton Mifflin, 1958). Shiloh is covered in Wiley Sword, *Shiloh: Bloody April* (New York: Morrow, 1974); and James L. McDonough, *Shiloh: In Hell before Night* (Knoxville: University of Tennessee Press, 1977); the Seven Days' Battles in Clifford Dowdey, *The Seven Days* (Boston: Little, Brown, 1964). Antietam is treated in J. V. Murfin, *The Gleam of Bayonets: The Battle of Antietam and the Maryland Campaign of 1862* (New York: T. Yoseloff, 1965); and S. W. Sears, *Landscape Turned Red: The Battle of Antietam* (New Haven: Ticknor & Fields, 1983).

Other western campaigns are handled well in memoirs and biographies of Beauregard, Bragg, Grant, Sherman, and George H. Thomas, but important views are offered in Thomas L. Connelly, *Army of the Heartland: The Army of Tennessee, 1861–1862* (Baton Rouge: Louisiana State University Press, 1967), and his *Autumn of Glory: The Army of Tennessee, 1862–1865* (Baton Rouge: Louisiana State University Press, 1971). Useful, too, are James L. McDonough, *Stones River: Bloody Winter in Tennessee* (Knoxville: University of Tennessee, 1980), and Stanley F. Horn, *The Army of Tennessee* (1953; Norman: University of Oklahoma Press, 1968). Sherman's march is recounted in John G. Barrett, *Sherman's March through the Carolinas* (Chapel Hill: University of North Carolina Press, 1956), and is recently examined in Joseph T. Glatthaar, *The March to the Sea and Beyond: Sherman's Troops in the Savannah & Carolina Campaigns* (New York: New York University Press, 1987).

The intricacies of Vicksburg are unscrambled in Samuel Carter III, *The Final Fortress: The Campaign for Vicksburg* (New York: St. Martin's Press, 1980); Earl Schenck Miers, *Web of Victory: Grant at Vicksburg* (New York: Knopf, 1955); Peter F. Walker, *Vicksburg: A People at War* (Chapel Hill: University of North Carolina Press, 1960).

Problems of Chattanooga operations are illustrated in Fairfax Downey, *Storming the Gateway: Chattanooga, 1863* (New York: D. McKay, 1969); and also in T. L Connelly's *Autumn of Glory,* cited earlier.

Virginia fighting from May, 1864, to the end is covered in biographies of Lee and Grant, but Bruce Catton's lyrical prose summons those last flashes of combat in *A Stillness at Appomattox* (Garden City, N.Y.: Doubleday, 1953). For Jubal Early's 1864 campaign to Washington, see Frank E. Vandiver, *Jubal's Raid: General Early's Famous At-*

tack on Washington in 1864 (New York: McGraw-Hill, 1960). For a brilliant account of operations at Petersburg, see Richard Sommers, *Richmond Redeemed: The Siege at Petersburg* (Garden City, N.Y.: Doubleday, 1981). Conditions in the contending armies have engaged the attention of many students. Preeminent among the studies on this complex subject are Bell I. Wiley, *The Life of Johnny Reb: The Common Soldier of the Confederacy* (Indianapolis: Bobbs-Merrill, 1943), and *The Life of Billy Yank: The Common Soldier of the Union* (Indianapolis: Bobbs-Merrill, 1952). Recent works are useful: Gerald Linderman, *Embattled Courage: The Experience of Combat in the American Civil War* (New York: Free Press, 1987); James I. Robertson, Jr., *Soldiers Blue and Gray* (Columbia: University of South Carolina Press, 1988); Reid Mitchell, *Civil War Soldiers: Their Expectations and Experiences* (New York: Viking, 1988); Randall C. Jimerson, *The Private Civil War: Popular Thought during the Sectional Conflict* (Baton Rouge: Louisiana State University Press, 1988).

Problems of conscription and desertion occupy a good number of volumes. Examples include Adrian Cook, *The Armies of the Streets: The New York City Draft Riots of 1863* (Lexington: University Press of Kentucky, 1974); Joseph Hernon, *Celts, Catholics, and Copperheads* (Columbus: Ohio State University Press, 1968). Wood Gray, *The Hidden Civil War: The Story of the Copperheads* (New York: Viking Press, 1942), highlights Democratic disloyalty to the Union, while Frank Klement in *The Copperheads in the Middle West* (Chicago: University of Chicago Press, 1960), and in *The Limits of Dissent: Clement L. Vallandigham and the Civil War* (Lexington: University Press of Kentucky, 1970), presents a more balanced view. Richard O. Curry, "The Union as It Was: A Critique of Recent Interpretations of the 'Copperheads,'" *Civil War History* 13 (1967): 25–39, doubts the depth of disloyalty. See also Ella Lonn, *Desertion during the Civil War* (Gloucester, Mass.: P. Smith, 1928); Bessie Martin, *Desertion of Alabama Troops from the Confederate Army* (New York: Columbia University Press, 1932); Albert B. Moore, *Conscription and Conflict in the Confederacy* (New York: MacMillan, 1924); Georgia L. Tatum, *Disloyalty in the Confederacy* (Chapel Hill: University of North Carolina, 1934). There is an active periodical literature on the subject of Confederate desertion, for which see Emory M. Thomas, *The Confederate Nation: 1861–1865* (New York: Harper & Row, 1979), pp. 352–53. For other areas of Confederate disaffection, see John B. Robbins, "The Confederacy and the Writ of *Habeas Corpus,*" *Georgia Historical Quarterly* 55 (1971), 83–101.

For the basic presentation of states' rights as a fatal Southern flaw, see Frank L. Owsley, *State Rights in the Confederacy* (Gloucester, Mass.: Peter Smith, 1925). An opposite view is given in May S. Ringold, *The Role of State Legislatures in the Confederacy* (Athens: University of Georgia Press, 1966). Resistance to Davis's programs by governors is well covered in Joseph H. Parks, *Joseph E. Brown of Georgia* (Baton Rouge: Louisiana State University Press, 1977); and Richard Yates, *The Confederacy and Zeb Vance* (Tuscaloosa, Ala.: Confederate Publishing Company, 1958).

Interior conditions in the wartime South are covered incisively in Charles W. Ramsdell, *Behind the Lines in the Southern Confederacy* (Baton Rouge: Louisiana State University Press, 1944); and Bell I. Wiley, *The Plain People of the Confederacy* (Baton Rouge: Louisiana State University Press, 1943). A first-person account is given in Mary B. Chesnut, *A Diary from Dixie,* ed. Ben Ames Williams (Boston: Houghton Mifflin, 1949). See also Louise B. Hill, *State Socialism in the Confederate States of America* (Charlottesville, Va.: Historical Publishing Company, 1936); Ella Lonn, *Salt as a Factor in the Confederacy* (University: University of Alabama, 1933); Mary E. Massey, *Ersatz in the Confederacy* (Columbia: University of South Carolina Press, 1952); Emory M. Thomas, *The Confederate State of Richmond: A Biography of the Capital* (Austin: University of Texas Press, 1971); George E. Turner, *Victory Rode the Rails: The Strategic Place of the Railroads in the Civil War* (Indianapolis: Bobbs-Merrill, 1953); Robert C. Black III, *The Railroads of the Confederacy* (Chapel Hill: University of North Carolina Press, 1952); Mary E. Massey, *Refugee Life in the Confederacy* (Baton Rouge: Louisiana State University Press, 1964), and *Bonnet Brigades* (New York: Knopf, 1966); Anne Firor Scott, *The Southern Lady: From Pedestal to Politics, 1830–1930* (Chicago: University of Chicago Press, 1970). Charles W. Ramsdell, among the most learned students of the Confederacy, wrote three seminal articles touching on specific phases of the Southern war economy: "The Confederate Government and the Railroads," *American Historical Review* 22 (1917), and "The Control of Manufacturing by the Confederate Government," *Mississippi Valley Historical Review* 8 (1921), and "General Robert E. Lee's Horse Supply, 1862–1865," *American Historical Review* 35 (1930).

The use of black troops and slaves in the contending armies is the subject of a burgeoning literature. For example: James M. McPherson et al., *Blacks in America* (Garden City, N.Y.: Doubleday, 1971); Eugene Genovese, *Roll, Jordan, Roll,* cited earlier; Clarence L. Mohr,

On the Threshold of Freedom: Masters and Slaves in Civil War Georgia (Athens: University of Georgia Press, 1986); Bell I. Wiley, *Southern Negroes, 1861–1865* (New York: Rinehart, 1938); James H. Brewer, *The Confederate Negro: Virginia's Craftsmen and Military Laborers, 1861–1865* (Durham, N.C.: Duke University Press, 1969); Robert F. Durden, *The Gray and the Black: The Confederate Debate on Emancipation* (Baton Rouge: Louisiana State University Press, 1972). For the use of black troops in the Union army, see Dudley T. Cornish, *The Sable Arm: Negro Troops in the Union Army, 1861–1865* (New York: Longmans, Green, 1956); James M. McPherson, *The Struggle for Equality: Abolitionists and the Negro in the Civil War and Reconstruction* (Princeton: Princeton University Press, 1964), and *The Negro's Civil War: How American Negroes Felt and Acted during the War for Union* (New York: Pantheon Books, 1965); Benjamin Quarles, *The Negro in the Civil War* (Boston: Little, Brown, 1953); Joseph T. Glatthaar, *Forged in Battle: The Civil War Alliance of Black Soldiers and White Officers* (New York: Free Press, 1990). Lawanda Cox defends Lincoln as a true advocate of black advancement in *Lincoln and Black Freedom: A Study in Presidential Leadership* (Columbia: University of South Carolina Press, 1981).

Technological issues are discussed in W. LeRoy Broun, "The Red Artillery," in *Southern Historical Society Papers* 26 (1898); L. Van Loan Naisawald, *Grape and Canister: The Story of the Field Artillery of the Army of the Potomac, 1861–1865* (New York: Oxford University Press, 1960); Jennings Cropper Wise, *The Long Arm of Lee: The History of the Artillery of the Army of Northern Virginia* (New York: Oxford University Press, 1959); Claude Fuller, *The Rifled Musket* (Harrisburg, Pa.: Stackpole Company, 1958); Josiah Gorgas, "Ordnance of the Confederacy, I, II," in *Army Ordnance* 16 (1936); Frank E. Vandiver, *Ploughshares into Swords: Josiah Gorgas and Confederate Ordnance* (Austin: University of Texas Press, 1952); Richard D. Goff, *Confederate Supply* (Durham, N.C.: Duke University Press, 1969); James L. Nichols, *The Confederate Quartermaster in the Trans-Mississippi* (Austin: University of Texas Press, 1964).

Naval matters are widely treated in the standard histories and especially in the pictorial collections. Among the most helpful specialized works are Virgil C. Jones, *The Civil War at Sea*, 3 vols. (New York: Holt, Rinehart Winston, 1960–62). H. A. Gosnell, *Guns on the Western Waters: The Story of River Gunboats in the Civil War* (Baton Rouge: Louisiana State University Press, 1949), treats a highly important sub-topic, as does Rowena Reed, *Combined Operations in the*

Civil War (Annapolis: Naval Institute Press, 1978); John T. Scharf, *History of the Confederate States Navy* (New York: Rogers & Sherwood, 1887); W. N. Still, *Confederate Shipbuilding* (Athens: University of Georgia Press, 1969), and *Iron Afloat: The Story of the Confederate Ironclads* (Nashville: Vanderbilt University Press, 1971); Tom H. Wells, *The Confederate Navy: A Study in Organization* (University: University of Alabama Press, 1971); Hamilton Cochran, *Blockade Runners of the Confederacy* (Indianapolis: Bobbs-Merrill, 1958); F. E. Vandiver, ed., *Confederate Blockade Running Through Bermuda, 1861–1865: Letters and Cargo Manifests* (Austin: University of Texas Press, 1947); Stephen R. Wise, *Lifeline of the Confederacy: Blockade Running during the War* (Columbia: University of South Carolina Press, 1988). An intriguing oddment of the naval war is the subject of Milton F. Perry's *Infernal Machines: The Story of Confederate Submarine and Mine Warfare* (Baton Rouge: Louisiana State University Press, 1965). A worthwhile memoir is Thomas E. Taylor, *Running the Blockade: A Personal Narrative of Adventures, Risks, and Escapes During the American Civil War* (London: J. Murray, 1897).

All readers on the war should begin with Stephen Vincent Benet's epic *John Brown's Body* (New York: Rinehart & Company, 1928), poetic history which distills the essence of the conflict for both North and South.

Index

Murfreesboro, Tenn., battle of, 124, 146
Myers, Gen. Abraham C., 78–80

Napoleon, 59, 60
Nashville, Tenn., battle of, 171
Nassau, Bahamas, 91
navy, Confederate, 50; amphibious operations of, 89; and blockade running, 91–92; and commerce raiders, 89–91; condition of, 87–88
navy, U.S.: amphibious operations of, 72, 84–85, 89, 108, 116, 121; and commerce raiders, 89–90; condition of, 83; construction program for, 83–84
Nebraska, 18, 34
Negroes. See blacks
Neosho, Mo., 95
neurasthenia, 155–56
Nevada, 96
New England Emigrant Aid Society, 35
New Mexico, campaign in, 96
New Orleans, La., 85, 121
Newsom, Ella King, 69
New York, 37
New York City, 10–11, 16, 58–59, 155
Nitre and Mining Bureau, 77
None Died in Vain (Leckie), 34
North Atlantic Blockading Squadron, 83
North Carolina, 50, 83
Northrop, Lucius Bellinger, 24, 78
Northwest Ordinance, 18
Nullification, 44

Oak Hill, Mo., battle of. See Wilson's Creek
Ohio, Department of the, 117
Olustee, Fla., battle of, 158
On War (Clausewitz), 59
Order of American Knights, 9
Ordnance Department, 76–78, 79, 80, 91
Osawatamie, Kans., 37
Outpost (Mahan), 59

Paludan, Phillip, quoted, 16, 54, 56, 60
pay, for Confederate troops, 79
Peace Convention, Washington, D.C., 45–46
Pea Ridge, Ark., battle of, 97

Pember, Phoebe, 69
Pemberton, Gen. John, 98; at Vicksburg, 138, 144–45
Pensacola, Fla., 48
"People's Contest, A" (Paludan), quoted, 16, 54
Perryville, Ky., battle of, 124
personal liberty laws, 32
Petersburg, Va.: railroads in, 65, 171; siege of, 78, 171–76
Philadelphia, Pa., 16
Pickens, Gov. Francis, 49
Pickett, Gen. George Edward, 139–41
Pigeon's Ranch, battle of. See Glorieta Pass, N.Mex.
Pike, Gen. Albert, 95
Pillow, Gen. Gideon, 94
Pinkerton, Allan, 45
Plains Indians, 95
planter class, 31
Pleasanton, Gen. Alfred, 138
Polk, Gen. Leonidas, 94
Pope, Gen. John, 12; army of, 110; at Cedar Mountain, 113; and Second Bull Run campaign, 113–14, 125
Porter, Gen. Fitz-John, 108–10
Port Hudson, Miss., 144
Port Republic, Va., battle at, 107
Port Royal, S.C., 72
"Prayer of Twenty Millions": Lincoln's reply to, 15–16
Price, Gen. Sterling, 95, 96, 97, 98
prisoners, exchange of, 166
Produce Loan, 78
Prosser, Gabriel, 39

Quartermaster Department, Confederate, 78–80; buys ships, 91

racism, 34
Radical republicans, 9, 56–57
railroads, 53, 54–56; at Chickamauga, 147–48; and Confederate management, 64–65, 165; and Confederate railroad bureau, 79; at First Bull Run (Manassas), 66; and Shiloh campaign, 118; southern, 63–65, 73, 154, 167
Rains, Col. George W., 76
Ramsdell, Charles W., 64, 74
Randolph, George W., 28, 114
reconstruction, 19

Blood Brothers was composed into type on a Compugraphic digital phototypesetter in eleven point Galliard with two points of spacing between the lines. Galliard was also selected for display. The book was designed by Jim Billingsley, typeset by Metricomp, Inc., and printed offset by Hart Graphics, Inc. The paperback books were bound by Hart Graphics, Inc. The cloth bound books were bound by John H. Dekker & Sons, Inc. The paper on which this book is printed carries acid-free characteristics for an effective life of at least three hundred years.

TEXAS A&M UNIVERSITY PRESS : COLLEGE STATION

Riverside
County

LIBRARY SYSTEM

www.rivlib.net